I Remember,
Daddy

I Remember, Daddy

Katie Matthews

The harrowing true story of a daughter haunted
by memories too terrible to forget

HARPER
element

This book is based on the author's experiences. In order to protect
privacy, some names, identifying characteristics, dialogue and details
have been changed or reconstructed.

HarperElement
An Imprint of HarperCollins*Publishers*
77–85 Fulham Palace Road,
Hammersmith, London W6 8JB

www.harpercollins.co.uk

and *HarperElement* are trademarks of
HarperCollins*Publishers* Ltd

First published by HarperElement 2011

1 3 5 7 9 10 8 6 4 2

A catalogue record of this book
is available from the British Library

ISBN 978-0-00-741902-9

Printed and bound in Great Britain by
Clays Ltd, St Ives plc

Mixed Sources

Product group from well-managed
forests and other controlled sources
www.fsc.org Cert no. SW-COC-001806
© 1996 Forest Stewardship Council

FSC is a non-profit international organisation established to promote the
responsible management of the world's forests. Products carrying the FSC
label are independently certified to assure consumers that they come
from forests that are managed to meet the social, economic and
ecological needs of present and future generations.

Find out more about HarperCollins and the environment at
www.harpercollins.co.uk/green

Acknowledgements

Sam – the one thing I did right in my life was to have you. You are my reason for living and I love you very much. You have grown into a lovely young man and I am so proud of you. Even though there were times when I wasn't well and I was unable to look after you, you were always in my thoughts and I am the luckiest mum alive to have you as my loving son.

Jenny – I don't really need to say much because you know. Thank you for the last 32 years, and here's to many more. I love you.

Megan – I hope that we have wine-o'clocks soon. I miss you.

Jack – you showed me how to love and how to be loved. Thank you for believing in me and for your wonderful sense of humour, which got me through many a dark day. For that alone I am eternally grateful.

To everyone who has been or is being abused – PLEASE tell someone. IT IS NOT YOUR FAULT. I hope that reading this book might help you in some way. I wish you peace and happiness. Don't be afraid to try to achieve your dreams – you can do it. You deserve the best, and you *are* worth it.

Lastly, to my father – this is closure for me. I cannot forgive you, but you no longer consume my life; you no longer scare me or have any hold over me. The unspeakable pain you caused me has made me stronger and I can honestly say now, 'Enough. I am done.'

One

The sound of Jackie's laugh was a distant, muffled echo, and as I tried to focus on her face, the room began to spin. Suddenly, I felt a sharp pain in my stomach, as though someone had stabbed me with the red-hot blade of a knife, and I gasped.

'Katie? Are you all right?' Jackie's voice came in waves, as though someone was placing a hand over the speaker on a radio and then lifting it away again. I tried to answer her, but it felt as though my tongue had swollen and was blocking off the back of my throat so that I could barely breathe. My whole body seemed heavy, and as I reached out my hand to try to steady myself on the reception desk, everything around me faded to blackness and I dropped to the ground like a puppet whose strings had been abruptly cut.

I don't know how long I'd been lying on the floor before I opened my eyes and saw the blurred image of Jackie's anxious face. She was leaning over me and her lips were moving, although all I could hear was the loud pulsing of blood in my head. I tried to sit up, but a firm hand on my shoulder pushed me gently down again, and then a voice that wasn't Jackie's said, 'Don't try to get up, Katie. You've had a nasty fall. Just lie still for a minute.'

And that was when the hammer started pounding violently in my head, making me feel sick and disorientated, so that it was a relief to lie back and feel the solid floor beneath the rough, ribbed-cord carpet. I closed my eyes, and when I opened them again, the room had finally stopped revolving and I could see more clearly both Jackie's face and that of another work colleague who was kneeling on the floor beside her.

As my senses gradually began to return, I became aware of a warm dampness that seemed to be seeping through the back of my skirt. The last thing I could remember was standing talking to Jackie, who'd been telling me something funny that had made us both laugh, and I supposed I must have been holding a cup of coffee, which I'd spilt when, presumably, I'd fainted.

Someone had placed a coat over me like a blanket, and I felt for the edge of it with my fingers and tried to say the word 'coffee'. But the only sound I made was a hoarse, unintelligible whisper. I swallowed and tried again, and this time Jackie leaned forward and gently covered my hand with the coat as she said, 'No, Katie. Don't have coffee now. Wait just a little while, until you're feeling better.'

I tried to shake my head, but the movement made the hammer inside it pound more vigorously, and so, for a moment, I lay completely still, waiting for the wave of nausea that was washing over me to recede. Then, twisting my shoulders so that I could reach down towards the hem of my skirt, I touched the dampness on my leg. I must have banged my arm on the reception desk as I fell, because a sharp pain like an electric shock shot from my elbow to my wrist. Again, I lay completely still, waiting for the worst of the pain to pass before I pulled my hand out slowly from beneath the coat and raised it in front of my face.

At first, I couldn't identify the dark stain on my fingers. It wasn't coffee, or even, as I'd been so afraid it might be, my own urine. And then I realised it was blood. A jolt of fear made my heart start to race and I felt a sense of total weariness. I rested my hand, palm upwards, on top of the coat that covered me and whispered Jackie's name.

'Yes, love,' she said immediately, leaning over me again and smiling a small, reassuring smile. 'I'm still here, Katie.'

At that moment, someone must have noticed the blood on my fingers, because a hand slowly lifted the edge of the coat and I heard a sharp intake of breath, followed by a man's voice saying, 'Oh my God! There's blood everywhere. It's all over her legs. Where's that sodding ambulance?'

Someone shushed him, and then Jackie put her hand on my arm. 'It's all right, Katie,' she said. 'You probably cut yourself when you fell. I expect you caught your leg on the side of the desk. We've called an ambulance just to be on the safe side, so that they can check you over and make sure you haven't broken anything. You're okay, though. You're going to be okay. Don't worry.'

But I could see clearly the worry in her eyes.

She stroked the top of my arm distractedly as she added, 'Someone's gone to find Tom. He'll be here any minute. You'll be all right, Katie.'

I wanted to tell her that they wouldn't find my boyfriend Tom, because he was out doing a delivery. But it suddenly felt as though a weight was pressing down on top of me, forcing the last few ounces of energy out of my body. So, instead, I just closed my eyes and let the hot tears run out between my eyelashes.

They didn't make contact with Tom before the ambulance arrived, so I went to the hospital alone. And as I lay in the emergency department, staring up at a

4

patch of flaking paint on the ceiling above my head, I tried not to be afraid.

It sounded as though a dozen people were all talking at once, and then someone laid a long-fingered hand on my arm and said, in a slow, precise voice, 'I'm sorry, Katherine. I'm afraid you may be losing the baby.'

Finally, I had something to focus on. But although I could understand each of the individual words the doctor had spoken, I couldn't make sense of what he'd actually said. I wiped my hand across my eyes, brushing away some of the tears that were wetting my hair and dampening the pillow under my head, and then I turned to look at the doctor.

'What baby? There *is* no baby. I can't …' I sobbed a single, choking sob and whispered, 'I was raped when I was 18. And I was … damaged. So I can't have a baby.'

'I'm sorry.' The doctor touched my arm again and I wondered for a moment whether he meant that he was sorry because I'd been raped or because he'd made a mistake about the baby I couldn't have. 'You're definitely pregnant, though,' he said. 'We need to take you up to the operating theatre to have a proper look.'

I felt the small knot of panic that had been lying like a lump of lead in my stomach start to unravel, sending expanding threads of fear up through my chest until I could taste its sourness in my mouth. I pressed my face into the pillow and, for a moment, thought about giving in to the miserable weariness that was threatening to overwhelm me, and sleep. Instead, though, I turned to look at the doctor again, reached out to touch his white-coated sleeve and said, 'Please try to save my baby.'

When I woke up from the anaesthetic, Tom was sitting beside the bed, his hand covering mine, and as I looked up into his eyes, I knew immediately that there *had* been a baby and that they hadn't managed to save it. I felt an almost physical sense of sadness and loss, which seemed out of all proportion for something I'd never really known I'd had. And as Tom leaned forward to touch my cheek with his fingers, I burst into tears and cried as though my heart had broken.

TWO

Tom worked in the despatch department of the company where I'd been working for the last few months. We'd fallen for each other almost as soon as we met, and within a few weeks I'd moved in to live with him at his mum and dad's house. That was the way I did everything in those days; I was impetuous and made quick decisions, determined to live my life to the full and to throw all my energy into doing the things I wanted to do. It was always all or nothing with me then, and I knew I'd been really lucky to find Tom. He was a shy, lovely guy, with a large, loving family that soon became the family I'd never really had.

Tom and I had been together just less than three months when I collapsed that day at work. We hadn't been using contraception, because I'd told him that I'd been raped when I was 18 and that, because of the damage that had been done to me, the doctor had said it was very unlikely I'd ever be able to have children. It was a sadness I thought I'd come to terms with, and Tom had seemed to accept it too. But, when I had the miscarriage and we lost the baby that day, I could tell he hadn't been as resigned to the prospect of not having children as he'd pretended.

On the day when I was taken to hospital after fainting at work, the doctor told me, 'You were about eight weeks' pregnant. Unfortunately, though, it was ectopic – the baby was growing outside your uterus. I'm afraid it never really stood a chance.'

It was a shock to discover that I could conceive after all, although there was still the possibility that I'd never be able to carry a baby to full term. And I was surprised, too, by the profound sense of grief I felt when I was told that I'd lost the baby I'd only known about for a matter of minutes. My reaction seemed to border on the self-pitying, and feeling sorry for yourself wasn't something that had been allowed by my father. No one likes a whinger, he'd told me more times than I could count. So, when things went wrong, I'd learned to pick myself up, dust myself off, and start all over again. Now, though, I felt as though I'd suffered a heart-breakingly important loss. And what also seemed particularly daunting and unnerving was the thought that I was going to have to reconsider all the assumptions I'd made about who I was and who I might be in the future.

Of more immediate and pressing concern, though, was the fact that I'd have to start using some sort of contraceptive. So, six weeks after I'd lost the baby that had been growing silently inside me, Tom drove me to the family-planning clinic.

I hated talking about sex at the best of times, and the knowledge that I was going to be asked personal questions by a total stranger made me feel quite sick. I didn't want Tom to come into the clinic with me, and I think he was vastly relieved when I asked him to wait outside in the van.

The nurse asked me all the questions I'd expected – about my health and my sex life – and then one I hadn't anticipated: 'Is there any possibility you might be pregnant?'

'Well, no,' I told her, shrugging slightly and wondering if she'd been listening to any of my answers to her previous questions. 'I told you, I've just lost a baby.'

She looked up at me, her pen paused above the folder on her desk and her head inclined at a slight angle, one eyebrow raised. Then she said slowly, 'The time when you're most likely to fall pregnant is when you've just lost a baby.'

'No one told me that!' I answered huffily.

'How old are you?' She looked down at the desk and shuffled her papers.

'Twenty-three,' I said, feeling suddenly unworldly and embarrassingly naïve.

'Well, let's do a quick pregnancy test, shall we?' She cleared her throat and then looked up at me again with an encouraging smile.

'But I'm only here to get the pill,' I protested.

'I know. That's fine. But we just need to make sure, to be on the safe side.' She stood up, collected together her papers and opened the door, and I followed her meekly into the corridor.

Half an hour later, I walked out of the clinic and into the car park, opened the door of Tom's van and climbed into the passenger seat beside him.

'Are you sitting down?' I asked Tom, stupidly.

'Well, of course I'm sitting down!' He turned to look at me with a quizzical expression. 'What is it, Katie? What's going on?'

'I'm pregnant,' I told him, staring out through the windscreen, but seeing nothing.

'What? You mean the baby's still there?' The distress in his voice made me turn to look at him at last, and I could see tears in his eyes as he reached for my hand and said, 'But you lost the baby. I don't understand.'

'This is another baby,' I told him. 'I'm pregnant *again*.'

We sat together in silence for a moment, both of us trying to absorb information that our minds didn't seem able to process.

'That's great,' Tom said at last, wiping the back of his hand quickly across his cheeks. 'It's great news. My mum and dad will be thrilled.'

'It isn't great news!' I almost shouted at him. 'I can't do this. I can't be pregnant. I'm all messed up inside. What if I lose this one too? I *won't* do this, Tom. I'm not prepared to take the risk.'

Tom was right about one thing, though: his parents *were* over the moon when they heard the news, and they were devastated when I told them I was going to have an abortion.

'Please,' his mother begged me. 'I know it's your life, Katie, and I understand that you haven't got over your recent loss. But ...' She hesitated, then took a deep breath and said, 'What if this is the only other chance to have a child you ever get? Don't throw it away. Please. It would be our first grandchild. You can't imagine how we've longed for this. We'll help you. I promise.'

I already felt a tremendous sense of guilt towards the child that was never going to be born, and now I also felt guilty about disappointing Tom's parents, who'd always been so kind and so good to me. But I knew I simply couldn't face going through with the pregnancy. I was obsessed with the thought of being able to feel the baby growing and developing inside me and then my body rejecting it, killing it instead of nurturing and protecting it. And there was something else that was worrying me, too. I often had fleeting impressions of my own childhood that I could never capture for long enough to be able to make sense of them, and although I didn't know what those unre-membered images were, I knew that somehow they were linked to my fear of being responsible for a child of my own.

I went for the obligatory counselling session and then booked an appointment to have an abortion. But when I woke up on the appointed morning, I phoned the clinic and said, 'I've changed my mind. I'm not coming. I can't do it.'

When I told Tom's parents that I'd cancelled my appointment, his dad mumbled something gruffly kind and patted my shoulder, and his mother envel-oped me in a warm, breath-expelling hug and, with tears in her eyes, repeated her promise that they'd help us in any way they could. And although none of us could have known it at the time, it was a promise for which I was one day going to be immeasurably grateful.

I had a horrendous pregnancy, and at about four months I fainted again. Tom was with me this time and he rushed me into hospital, weaving through the traffic and sounding the horn of his van in a way I'd never seen him do before. Despite his efforts, though, I was bleeding by the time we reached the hospital, and the doctor told me I was going into early labour. It seemed that all my worst nightmares were coming true. I'd been so afraid of being pregnant and of becoming a parent that I'd almost had an abortion. But I'd changed my mind, because, in the end, my own fears hadn't seemed to constitute an adequate reason for snuffing out a life that was only just beginning. And it was only then, when I'd made the decision to go ahead with the pregnancy, that I'd realised how desperately I wanted the child that was growing inside me. I knew Tom wanted it too, and that he'd tried to convince himself that he'd come to terms with the possibility of never having a son or daughter of his own simply because he loved me.

What made what was happening even more difficult to bear was the fact that I thought I was almost through the most dangerous period of my pregnancy, and I'd only just dared to allow myself to start believing that I might actually be going to carry my baby to full term. For the last few weeks, I'd felt sick most of the time, and although the constant nausea and occasional bouts of vomiting were really hard to live with every day, I'd comforted myself with the thought that perhaps they were good signs, because at least they probably meant that my hormones were doing what they ought to be doing.

In the hospital, they gave me drugs to try to prevent my going into labour prematurely. I knew that babies born at four months couldn't survive, and it was clear that they didn't really hold out much hope. But, by some miracle, the contractions gradually became less frequent and finally stopped, and the following day I was allowed to go home.

Everything seemed to settle down after that. The rest of my pregnancy was relatively uneventful and I went into labour two weeks after my due date.

The labour itself was horrible. Tom held my hand, wiped away the sweat that was streaming out of every pore in my body, and counted '*In* – two – three; *out* – two – three – four,' as I tried to breathe away the pain and suppress the panic. But it soon became clear that no amount of controlled breathing was going to push the baby out of my body, and I was given a spinal block so that it could be literally dragged out of me with forceps. And, ironically, it was at that point that Tom forgot to follow the breathing technique he'd been counting out so carefully for me, and he fainted and had to be half-carried out of the room. Which meant that, sadly, he wasn't there to see our child emerge into the world or to hear its first feeble cry.

Immediately the baby was born, it was whisked away to a corner of the delivery room, and I lay back, exhausted, on the bed, listening and waiting for the more vigorous wailing I knew would begin as soon its tiny lungs had filled with air.

The seconds and then the minutes ticked by, and still the only sounds I could hear were the hushed, urgent voices of the doctor and one of the nurses. Eventually, I lifted my head to try to see what they were doing, and – because, for some reason, no one had thought to tell me – asked, 'Is it a boy or a girl?'

For a moment, no one answered. Then a nurse walked towards me, placed a tightly wrapped bundle on my chest and said, 'It's a boy,' and I looked down for the first time into the huge blue eyes and wrinkled, blue-tinged face of my son.

The doctor came and stood beside the bed. 'He's having some problems breathing,' he told me. 'We need to get him into intensive care.' He leaned towards me and reached out to lift the baby from my arms, and I just had time to touch the skin of my son's cheek and whisper 'Hello' before he was rushed out of the room.

Because of the spinal anaesthetic I'd been given, I had to lie flat on my back for the next 24 hours, which meant that I couldn't get out of bed to have a shower, and when my mother came in to see me, she took one look at my tangled, matted hair, said, 'Look at the state of you!' and burst into tears. It wasn't the greeting I'd expected, but I think she'd been more worried about me and about the baby than I'd realised.

For the next few minutes, she concentrated on getting me tidied up and 'presentable', which was probably her way of dealing with the sudden rush of relief and emotion she was feeling.

As soon as I was able to get out of bed, I had a wash and waited for my son to be brought in to me so that I could feed him. When the nurse handed him to me, I felt nervous and excited. I pulled back the edge of the blanket the baby was wrapped in and looked down into a huge, moon-like face framed by a shock of bright red hair.

'This isn't my child!' I told the nurse.

'Of course he's your child,' she said. Her tone was briskly coaxing, as though she was speaking to a small child or a very stupid adult. Then she gave a quick, nervous laugh and patted my shoulder as she added, 'Who else's child would he be? Isn't he just the spitting image of his father?'

'I don't know,' I said. 'He may well look *exactly* like his father.' I spoke slowly, trying to control the hysteria and panic that were rising up inside me. 'But I've never seen his father, because this isn't my child. My child doesn't have red hair and he's less than half the size of this baby.'

'There, there.' The nurse's tone was so patronisingly patient that I had a strong, but mercifully fleeting, desire to throw the baby at her. She looked at me warily, patted my shoulder again and assured me, 'He *is* your baby. There's no question about that.'

Suddenly, all the pain, worry and exhaustion of the last few hours hit me with full force and I burst into tears. I didn't have the strength to argue with her, but I knew that if I didn't, I was going to go home with someone else's baby – and, even more importantly, someone else was going to go home with mine.

At that moment, another nurse strode purposefully down the ward towards us, holding another, slightly smaller, white bundle in her arms.

'Well, here we are, Mummy!' she said, in a no-nonsense, nursery-teacher's voice. 'Here's your little one all ready for his first feed.'

As she spoke, she reached across and almost snatched the red-haired monster of a baby from my arms, deftly replacing him with my son. Then both nurses turned and scuttled away, and I looked down for the second time at my baby and couldn't believe how beautiful he was.

When Tom came into the hospital later that day, he was like the cat that got the cream. I was touched by his obvious and immediate love for his son, and by his gratitude to me for having given him the child he could only now admit to having wanted.

Over the next couple of days, we tried to decide on a name. While I was pregnant, we'd already narrowed down our choices of boys' names to either Daniel or Richard. But the more we looked at our baby, the less the names seemed to suit him, and eventually we agreed on Sam. I wasn't sure whether he really looked like a Sam, but everyone else seemed to think he did, and as it was a name I liked, and one that had no negative associations for either of us, I was happy to agree to it.

Strangely, it seemed that as soon as he had a name, Sam had his own identity. It was a thought that, for some reason, sent a bolt of pain through my heart. And then I realised that what I was feeling wasn't pain but fear: I was afraid of the enormity of being responsible for a life that was already far more precious to me than anyone else's, including my own.

At visiting time the next day, the double doors at the end of the maternity ward crashed open and I looked up to see my father striding towards me. He was almost completely hidden behind a huge bouquet of flowers and his girlfriend, Gillian, was scurrying along behind him, looking tentative and hesitant.

I glanced anxiously at my mother, silently cursing my father for flaunting Gillian in front of her in a clearly deliberate act of spite that was completely out of place at what should have been a family time. My mother took a step away from my bed and started fussing with her handbag, as though to indicate that she had no intention of trying to fight for her rightful place in the pecking order.

'So, what are you calling it?' my father bellowed, leaning down towards me and offering his cheek for me to kiss. The whole ward had fallen silent. Even the sucking sounds made by the newborn babies when they were feeding and their gentle murmuring when they weren't seemed momentarily to have stopped. Everyone's eyes were on my father. Some people were regarding him with open admiration, and some were watching him with expressions of hostile disapproval at the loudness of his self-assurance. But it was clear that all of them were impressed, despite themselves.

'We've decided to call him Sam,' I told my father, reaching out to place a subconsciously protective hand on the cot beside the bed.

'Sam!' My father almost spat out the word in disgust. 'What sort of a name is Sam for Christ's sake? It's a fucking dog's name. I thought you'd call him Harold, after me and after my father. You're fucking useless.'

Then, without even glancing towards his first-born grandchild, he threw the ridiculously ostentatious bouquet of flowers on to the bed, turned on his heels, barked 'Gillian!' and marched back down the ward, letting the doors swing shut behind him.

My father didn't see Sam again until he was nine months old. But, by that time, everything had changed, nothing would ever be the same again, and I could hardly bear to watch him put his hands on my beloved son.

Three

Although I'd had little contact with my father for several years by the time I discovered I was pregnant with Sam, and he didn't play much of a role in my life, it had been a few weeks before I'd plucked up the courage to tell him. I knew he thought Tom wasn't 'good enough' for me – which was particularly ironic considering the fact that his own background had been even more humble than Tom's. But, whereas Tom was perfectly comfortable in his own skin, my father had spent years climbing the social ladder, and he was proud that he'd 'risen above' his early life on a council estate and become a wealthy, successful and powerful businessman. Status, money and appearances were all that mattered to him, which was why, when I did finally tell him I was pregnant, I was surprised that he declared himself to be pleased and said he was looking forward to becoming a grandfather for the first time. Clearly, though, any grandfatherly feelings he might have had had evaporated that day he came to the hospital, when he decided that the name of my child mattered more than the child himself.

Tom and I had taken out a mortgage and bought a house together when I was four months' pregnant. Although I'd been happy living with Tom's parents, having a place of my own was really important to me. I'd bought my first flat when I was just 21 and was working as the manageress of a shop. It was a financial stretch on the salary I was earning, but it was worth it. I'd furnished it with bits of furniture my dad had been going to throw out, and I'd painted the walls, put curtains up at the windows and kept it spotlessly clean. I was really proud of that flat, partly, I think, because it seemed like a visible representation of the fact that I'd overcome the problems I'd had as a teenager and had proved my teachers – and my father – wrong by actually achieving something. It was the first place I'd ever lived where I felt safe, because I knew that I could close my own front door and choose who I invited into my home, and into my life. I'd had a horrible childhood and, until I bought that flat, nothing I'd ever done had felt as though it was my choice.

I Remember, Daddy

As a child, every aspect of my life had been entirely controlled by my father, and even as an adult I still felt the effect of his influence in many ways. My father's parents had had very little money when he was growing up, but he'd worked hard to become a well-off, successful businessman and he was so determined to *be* someone that he didn't care what it took for him to achieve that goal.

He had two sides to his character. To his friends he was eccentric, fun-loving and flamboyant, an amusing raconteur who had a way with the ladies and was the generous host of countless extravagant parties. To his family, however, he was a frightening, self-centred, violent alcoholic, a strict disciplinarian who despised women, hated foreigners, Catholics, poor people, homeless people, people who showed weakness or inadequacy in any way, people who smoked ... The list was almost endless.

He regularly abused my mother, both mentally and physically, bullied and beat my brother and me, and cast a shadow over my childhood from which I never truly emerged. By the time he and my mother divorced, when I was seven, the damage he had done to me seemed irreversible: I was a nervous, bewildered, insecure little girl without one scrap of self-confidence, who became a deeply depressed and confused teenager.

My mother was a shy, pretty young woman who'd had a sheltered upbringing in an affluent family, and who'd grown up to be both naïve and unsure of herself. When she met my extrovert, confident, flamboyant father, she was swept off her feet, overwhelmed by him, and she fell madly in love. She was devastated when she found him in bed with another woman on the night before their wedding. But he could talk his way out of any situation, however incriminating it might seem, and she really did love him. So she forgave him and married him anyway. And it was only after they were married that she began to realise that the man who had seemed so loving and caring was, in reality, a self-centred, violent bully with an almost inexhaustible and perverted sexual appetite.

My father had always been a heavy drinker who progressed through various stages of drunkenness. During the first stage, he'd be charming and affectionate and he'd tell exaggerated stories that made everyone laugh and say to each other what a great bloke he was. But the final stage – which usually didn't start until he was alone at home with my mother – was at completely the other end of the spectrum, and he'd be vicious, aggressive and frightening.

It was the early 1960s when my parents got married and, even had my mother been able to pluck up the courage to leave my father when she began to discover what he was really like, her parents – as well as everyone else who knew her – would have been totally horrified by the idea of a divorce. And, unfortunately, unlike my father – who was ruthlessly determined to do and to have whatever he wanted, and apparently completely indifferent to what other people might think – my mother was timidly anxious to do the right thing, and she would never have considered bringing such shame on herself or on her family.

After my parents were married, my mother worked to support my father through university. She didn't earn very much, but just four years after my father graduated, they were able to move with their newborn son into a five-storey house in one of the most prestigious addresses in town. And that's where they were living when I was born, a couple of years later.

The house was huge. It had a large, old-fashioned kitchen in the semi-basement, with a range cooker, an enormous pantry and an adjoining laundry room. Above it, on the ground floor, were the family living rooms, although it was the dining and drawing rooms on the first floor that were most impressive. They were furnished with beautiful, polished antique furniture and oil paintings in elaborately carved and moulded frames, and their high ceilings and tall, elegantly proportioned windows looked out on to the leafy square across the road.

My father loved paintings, and there were two in particular that I remember. One of them was of him as a child, aged seven years old, and the other was of his mother. The painting of my father was in a heavy gilt frame, with his name, age and the date engraved on a plaque at the bottom. It hung on the wall above the Georgian fireplace in the drawing room – and in equally prominent positions in every other house he ever lived in. I don't know whether it was actually painted when he was a child. Apart from the fact that his parents had very little money, they didn't really seem to be the sort of people who would commission an oil painting of their son – however much his mother might have adored him. Perhaps my father had had it painted himself, from a photograph, when he was an adult. Having a portrait in oils of himself as a child would have fitted in with his aspirations to become someone of substance and with his idea of who he really was – or who he felt he should have been.

My father was very strict with me and my brother Ian, and I don't remember him ever playing with us or taking us out anywhere when we were children. When he wasn't at work, out playing tennis or socialising, he was sleeping, and he had no time and certainly no inclination to bother much with us. In any case, he believed that children should be seen as little as possible and never heard. So he rarely spoke to us, although he shouted at us constantly, particularly at my brother, who he called a wimp and a cry-baby.

My mother used to try to hustle us out of the way as soon as she heard him coming home from work. Then he'd vent his bad temper on her instead – and it did seem as though he was almost always in a bad temper when there was no one else in the house except us. He'd criticise my mother and sneer at her until he reduced her to tears, and as soon as she was crying, he'd be more annoyed than ever.

He was totally different with other people, though. He had a loud, infectious laugh and could be charming when he wanted to be; and he loved giving parties. So, while my brother and I were looked after by the au pair of the moment, my mother would shop, cook and clean and then fix her hair and make-up, put on a pretty dress and smile as she handed round food to my father's friends and colleagues, their wives and girlfriends.

Despite his love of parties, however, my father didn't believe in celebrating our birthdays or even Christmas – I can't remember one single Christmas Day of my childhood – and he didn't believe in presents. On the one occasion when I did have a birthday party, all the gifts that had been bought for me were collected into black bin bags as soon as the guests had gone home, and then they were given away.

The only time my father showed any interest in me and my brother was when he made us perform for the entertainment and amusement of his guests. We were like little puppets, only really coming to life in my father's eyes when he decided to tug at our strings and show us off. From the time I was three years old, he used to teach me fables in French, which I had to recite on demand to his friends. They'd all stand around me in a circle, sipping their whisky from crystal glasses and smiling benevolently as I spouted words I didn't understand, which my father had taught me, parrot-fashion.

I can't remember the fables now, although I *can* still remember clearly how afraid I used to be of my father's sudden impatient anger whenever I made a mistake while he was teaching them to me. I can remember how my whole body used to shake and how I'd clench my little fists until my hands were damp with sweat and my fingernails were digging into my palms, and how my father towered over me like the embodiment of a threat as the strange, incomprehensible sounds tumbled from my lips. The fear I felt was well founded, because if I made just one mistake, my father would tell me to pull down my pants and lie across my bed and then he'd beat me with his belt, shouting at me that I was useless, before sending me to bed without any supper.

I Remember, Daddy

One of my earliest memories is of something that happened just before I turned three. My brother and I weren't allowed in the rooms on the first floor of the house. We had a playroom on the floor above, which was the only place we were supposed to play. But, when my father was at work, my mother used to let us do more or less what we wanted, and one day we decided to play trains in the drawing room. Ian was leading the way, making a very satisfactory steam-train noise, and I was holding on to his waist, following behind him and singing out 'Oooh-Oooh' every few minutes, in a not quite so realistic imitation of a train's whistle.

Suddenly, Ian tripped and fell headlong against one of the huge windows. There was an ear-splitting roar as the glass cracked and then dropped, in a massive sheet, to the ground, only just missing decapitating him. I screamed, but Ian just stood there in silence, too shocked to react. After a few seconds, he touched his hand to his forehead and looked at the blood on his fingers as though he couldn't understand what it was.

I was still screaming when I heard my father shout and, at the same moment, the drawing-room door flew open and he burst into the room, followed closely by my mother.

We found out later that he'd been walking home along the edge of the leafy square when he'd seen my brother fall against the window and had watched as the glass splintered and smashed. But, instead of being concerned about the long, deep gash on my brother's head, which was now spurting forth what looked like pints of blood, or about the fact that Ian had come very close to being killed, my father was almost ballistic with fury because we'd been playing in the drawing room.

Ian was still standing, dazed and completely still, near the empty window frame when my father came into the room. Finally, though, as the initial numbness of the shock began to wear off, his whole body started to shake violently. And it was at that moment that my father almost ran across the room and grabbed him by the shoulders.

'What the fuck are you doing in here?' he bellowed into my brother's blood-covered face. 'You are *not* allowed to play in the drawing room!' With each shouted word, he punched Ian on the arm and then he screamed, 'How many times do you have to be told something as simple as that?'

My brother flinched and leaned away from him.

'Please, Harry,' my mother said, touching my father's shoulder and then quickly pulling her hand away again. 'We need to get Ian to the hospital. It's a really serious cut.'

'The hospital?' My father's face was a deep-red colour and I knew he was on the verge of losing control completely. 'The fucking hospital?' he shrieked again. 'Get to your room! Both of you!' He swung round, took a step towards where I was cowering on the floor at the side of the chintz-covered sofa and shouted, '*Now!*'

As I fled from the room, I heard my mother pleading with him again, 'Please, Harry.' Then she gave a sharp cry, and I knew my father had punched her.

I sat on my bed, sobbing with shocked distress because of what had happened and because I was terrified of what was to come. A few minutes later, my father walked into my bedroom and slowly undid the buckle of his belt. Without having to be told, I pulled my pants down to my knees and lay on my stomach across my bed while he gave me 'ten of the best'. Then I struggled to my feet and tried to pull my pants back up over the bleeding rawness of my buttocks.

'Go to your brother's room.' My father spat the words at me, his face a contorted mask of hatred and fury.

I limped along the corridor and stood helplessly beside Ian, who was sitting on his bed crying, his tears diluting the blood that was still seeping from the cut on his head.

When I looked up, my father was standing in the doorway, surveying us both with an expression of disgust. 'You will stay there without food or water until Monday morning,' he said coldly, and then he turned and left the room, locking the door behind him.

It was a Friday evening. But I was just two years old and Ian was five, and we had no concept of how long it was until Monday.

A little while later, my mother came into the room carrying a tray of sandwiches and two glasses of water. As soon as she opened the door, my father appeared behind her, as if by magic.

'I thought I had made it clear that you are not to give them anything to eat or drink,' he said, in a slow, menacing voice.

My mother was startled by his silent, abrupt appearance and as she spun round to face him, one of the glasses tipped over, sending water cascading on to the sandwiches. She righted the glass and blinked rapidly as she pleaded with my father, 'Please, Harry. They're only children. They've got to eat. At least let them drink something. They can't stay locked in here without food or water for two whole days.'

Suddenly, without any warning, my father lashed out and hit her across the face, and she dropped the tray at his feet.

'Pick it up!' he hissed at her.

He kicked her as she fell to her knees and began to scoop up soggy pieces of sandwich and the two empty glasses. Then she stumbled out of the room and my father followed her, locking the door behind him, while we sat and listened to the sound of his footsteps fading away along the corridor.

Over the next two days and three nights, my brother and I played games together, cried when the pain of hunger and thirst grew too urgent to ignore, and slept for increasingly long periods of time. My mother came to check on us at irregular intervals, looking anxiously at the cut on my brother's head each time, before letting us out of the room to go to the toilet. Then she hugged us quickly, glancing over her shoulder with fearful eyes, and told us not to cry because it wouldn't be long before we could have something to eat.

During that weekend, we learned the price to be paid for disobeying my father. It was a lesson I always remembered every time I noticed the scar on my brother's head, although, in reality, it had been the cause of far worse scars for both of us that no one could see.

The kitchen in our house was overrun with mice, and as my father hated animals of all species, particularly anything small and scurrying, he used to make my brother or me go down to get ice-cream for him when he came home drunk at night or at the weekends. I'd have hated going down there in the dark even without the mice to contend with, but they terrified me.

I'd edge my way down the stairs and then grope frantically in the darkness for the switch that would light up the corridor leading to the kitchen. My heart would be thumping against my ribs and I'd have to cross my legs to stop the pee escaping as I forced myself to stand my ground and fumble for the light switch. Sometimes, I'd have to make several attempts, running back up the stairs and waiting in the light of the hallway each time while I summoned the courage to try again.

As I finally approached the kitchen door, I'd hear little feet scuttling on the flagstones and I'd stamp my own feet and bang my hands on the walls of the corridor. Then I'd stand still for a few moments to give the mice time to scamper back to their hiding places. But I didn't dare delay too long, because I knew my father would be waiting with increasingly impatient irritation for his ice-cream, and I was even more afraid of my father than I was of the mice.

Eventually, with one final thump on the kitchen door, I'd push it open and shudder at the sight of the thin, hairless tails of the last few mice as they shot behind the dresser or through the ragged-edged holes in the skirting board. Then I'd open the door of the freezer compartment in the fridge and scoop ice-cream into a bowl, singing or talking loudly to myself all the time so that the watching, waiting mice wouldn't think I'd gone and come darting back out again from their hiding places.

I dreaded those forays down to the kitchen, and I've been frightened of mice ever since. But I longed to have a hamster and, much to amazement, when I was five years old, my father agreed to let my mother buy one for me.

I adored Daisy from the moment I set eyes on her. She had to be kept in the laundry room next to the kitchen, although sometimes, when my father was at work, my brother and I would take her out of her little cage and carry her into the living room. We'd hold her and stroke her and let her run along the coffee table beside the couch and then I'd scoop her up again and try to kiss her pink, twitching, inquisitive little nose.

One day, when we'd taken Daisy into the living room, she escaped and, with our hearts racing, Ian and I were still searching for her when my father came home from work unexpectedly. As soon as we heard his tread on the stairs, we rushed to take our places on the sofa, and when the living-room door flew open, we were sitting the way our father always insisted we should sit – hands in our laps, backs ramrod straight. Except that, on this occasion, my hands were clasped

together so tightly I could feel the blood pulsing painfully in my wrists.

I prayed a silent prayer, although I had little hope of
it being heard by the unforgiving God whose terrible
wrath my grandmother had described to me so often
and in such frightening detail.

'Please,' I kept repeating over and over in my head.
'Please don't let Daddy see Daisy. Please keep her
hidden, just till he's left the room. I'll be good for ever
and ever. I promise.'

I knew we'd broken the rules by taking the hamster
into the living room. But I'd felt sorry for her, all alone
and cold in the laundry room, and I'd been certain
we'd hear my father's key turn in the lock of the front
door and would have plenty of time to slip down the
back stairs and return Daisy to her cage before he'd
even crossed the hallway.

Suddenly, out of the corner of my eye, I saw a flash
of white as the hamster ran along the arm of the chair
beside me. I glanced up quickly at my father, hoping
he hadn't noticed. But, although the expression on his
face barely changed, I knew that he had.

I held my breath, closing my eyes and sending tears
spilling out on to my cheeks as I waited for the
outburst of anger I knew was coming. To my astonish-
ment, however, my father remained silent, and after a
few seconds I dared to look up at him again. He was

standing with his back to the window, his mouth twisted into a tight line of distaste as he surveyed my brother and me coldly.

Then, spitting out the words with staccato finality, he spoke directly to me as he said, 'Take that thing back to where it belongs.'

I scooped the warm, furry body into my hands and ran from the room before he had time to change his mind. I could hardly believe what had happened. Had we really escaped the agonising lashings that were our usual punishment for any act of disobedience or sign of inadequacy? As the evening wore on and my father stayed locked in his study, it seemed that we had.

The next morning, when I crept into the kitchen for breakfast, my father didn't look up from his newspaper. I slid silently on to a chair, taking more than usual care to prevent it scraping noisily on the flagstone floor. Then I reached out my hand towards the silver toast rack – and screamed. Squashed into a milk bottle, just a few inches from my plate, was the twisted, suffocated little body of my hamster.

My father lowered his newspaper and leaned across the table towards me. His face was contorted into an ugly expression of vengeful satisfaction as he said, in a slow, even drawl, 'And that's what happens when you don't do what you're told.'

I was heartbroken. My whole body was shaking and I felt sick with shock and with the knowledge that the horrible death my little hamster had suffered had been *my* fault. If I hadn't broken the rules, Daisy would still be scuttling around happily in her cage. And, in that moment, I knew that my father was right: I was worthless and bad, because by not doing what I'd been told, I'd killed her.

Four

The first time I remember my father hitting me with his belt was when I was two years old. I soon learned that his word was law. If I didn't do what he told me to do, it was as though something snapped inside him and, whatever his mood had been, it would change instantly to one of blind, raging fury. Nothing ever excuses hitting a child, and it's beyond belief that anyone could bring themselves to thrash a two-year-old with a belt. But, as my father was only ever really physically violent towards me when I disobeyed him, I thought that *his* anger was *my* fault.

He didn't need a reason to punch my mother, though, or to attack her viciously; he sometimes did it just to make it clear to her – and perhaps to my brother and me, too – that he was in charge. And there was certainly no doubt in any of our minds that he *was* in charge, totally and utterly. It seemed that he controlled every breath we took, and I learned always to think about whether something I was going to do might make him angry, which meant that I lived in a constant state of almost unbearable anxiety.

To my father, my brother and I were nuisances who had to be taught to respect and obey him, but could otherwise be ignored. I think his only reason for having children at all was because it fitted in, peripherally, to his idea of the life he aspired to as a successful businessman living in an expensive house in an affluent and prestigious neighbourhood, with an attractive wife from a good family, and children who could recite poems and fables in French to order before they were whisked away out of sight by their nanny.

Surprisingly, perhaps, of all the countless things that hurt and terrified me during my childhood, it was often my father's violent bullying of my mother that was more frightening than anything else, and there were many occasions when I thought he was going to kill her.

One night, when I was five years old, I was woken up by the sound of someone sobbing. I lay on my back in my bed, listening, and after a few moments I realised that it was my mother. I released the breath I'd been holding – and, with it, a small, frightened whimper

— and then I started to count. One, two, three … When I got to ten it would stop, and if it hadn't … I paused in my counting and listened again.

Perhaps my parents were playing a game. I'd heard my mother shout out in the night before, and when I asked her about it the next morning, she told me that she and my father had just been 'messing around'. So, maybe, if I listened for long enough, I'd hear her laugh and then I'd know that everything was all right.

But, in my fiercely thumping heart, I knew it wasn't a game.

I heard my father shout something harsh and angry; then my mother cried out again, and this time there was no mistaking the terror in her voice. I pulled the bedcovers over my head, trying to block out the sound, and attempted to swallow the solid ball of fear that had lodged in my throat. I knew, though, that I couldn't just abandon my mother when she might need help.

I squeezed my eyes tightly shut for a moment and then, in one quick movement, sat up and swung my legs over the side of the bed. Then I tiptoed out of my room and crept along the thickly carpeted landing, counting my footsteps silently in my head to try to focus on something other than my own fear.

Crouching at the top of the stairs, I pushed my head just far enough through the balusters to be able to see my parents, who were standing on the staircase between the ground and first floors. My father was wearing a suit, but the top button of his shirt was undone, his tie was loose and askew and there was something about the way he looked that made me realise he was well past all of the first stages of drunkenness.

My mother was standing a couple of steps above him, wearing only a nightdress, and the fingers of my father's left hand seemed to be twisted in her hair. He was pulling her head backwards and punching her repeatedly on the side of her head, while she tried to cling on to the banister with one hand and protect herself against his blows with the other.

For a moment, I was transfixed by the sound of my father's humourless laugh, the cruel, thin-lipped expression on his upturned face and the brutal force of his attack on my mother. Then I noticed a young woman standing at the foot of the stairs. She was dressed in a short black skirt and a low-cut, wine-red-coloured sequined top and she was looking up towards my parents with a small, vague smile.

I felt a wave of relief. Clearly, it was some sort of game after all, because I knew that no adult would simply stand and watch without intervening while my father beat up my mother.

Suddenly, my father ripped his fingers out of my mother's hair, placed his hands against her shoulders, and gave her one hard push. As she fell backwards, her scream drowned out the sound of my own as I stumbled down the staircase towards her.

When I reached the bottom of the stairs, my mother was lying motionless on the marble-tiled floor of the hall. I was certain she was dead. I threw myself on to my knees beside her, calling 'Mummy! Mummy!' and gripping her shoulders with my hands as I tried to shake life into her.

The young woman had taken a step backwards, away from the foot of the stairs, as my mother fell, and she was teetering unsteadily on her stiletto heels towards the living room when my mother moaned and moved her head. The woman stopped, swaying slightly as she turned to face us again, and at that moment my father took one bound down the stairs, grabbed my arm and pulled me roughly to my feet.

'Get up! Get on your feet,' he shouted at my mother. 'There's nothing wrong with you. And maybe next time you hear me come home with a guest, you'll stay in bed and mind your own fucking business. *I* will decide who I entertain and who I bring into this house, and if you don't like it, you can fuck off.'

He leaned down, grabbed my mother under her arms and lifted her into an almost-standing position. Then he half-carried, half-dragged her through the hall and propped her up against the wall beside the front door. She staggered and almost fell, and I ran to her side and tried to put my arm around her waist.

'Go on, get out!' my father shouted, flinging the door wide open. 'Both of you!'

The snow that had started to fall before I went to bed that evening was still drifting silently and steadily from the sky. It had already covered the road and pavement outside the house with a layer of white that sparkled in the light from the open doorway. My mother looked at my father and I could tell that she was trying with all her might not to cry, because she knew her tears would only irritate him even more.

'Please, Harry,' she pleaded. 'You *can't* throw us out in the snow in just our nightdresses.'

'I can do what I bloody want,' my father shouted at her. 'Perhaps you should have thought about the snow before you tried to interfere.'

He grasped my mother's wrist as he spoke, put his other, open, hand on my back and shoved us out into the dark, freezing night. And as my bare feet touched the icy snow, I heard the front door slam and the key turn in the lock.

I was shaking uncontrollably and I felt my mother wince as I tightened my grip around her waist. But, despite the pain she must have been suffering as a result of her fall down the stairs, she raised her arm, placed it around my shoulders and held me tightly against her own shivering body.

We spent that night at a neighbour's house and, as I fell asleep, I remember wondering if the soles of my feet would ever stop burning.

I didn't know who the young woman was, whose company my father had chosen that night over my mother's. I doubt whether he even knew himself, or cared. He'd picked her up in a bar somewhere in town and she was gone in the morning, by the time my father let my mother and me return to the house.

My mother had had a comfortable upbringing, protected from the harsher realities of some people's lives. Her father had inherited a business that had been started by his grandfather and great-uncle, and she'd grown up leading the sort of life my father had been so determined to create for himself. However, her parents were sternly religious and firmly believed that children should learn to stand on their own two feet, which is why my mother had already been working when she met my father. I think she had little, if any, of her own money left by the time I was born; although she did still own a house near the coast, which we'd go to sometimes in the school holidays.

Years after it had happened, my mother told me about something my father had done one night when we were staying at that house. My parents left me and my brother with a babysitter and went out to a dinner-dance. It was an event that was linked in some way to my father's business and he was fussing and shouting even before they left the house. Despite being bullied and constantly told to hurry up, my mother always looked beautiful when she was dressed up to go out in the evening, and I used to love the light, flowery smell of perfume that lingered in my bedroom for a while after she'd come in to say goodnight.

It was winter and snowing again, and on the way back from the dinner my father was driving slowly through the deserted, snow-covered lanes when he got angry about something and started to shout at my mother. Suddenly, he slammed on the brakes and told her to get out of the car. She was wearing high-heeled shoes made of embroidered satin, a full-length ball gown and a short fur jacket that was designed more for decorative than for practical purposes of providing warmth and protection from the elements.

'Please, Harry,' she begged. 'We're at least three miles from home. I'll freeze to death, and I can't walk in these shoes.'

'Well, take them off then,' my father bellowed, leaning across her to open the passenger door and pushing her out on to the snow at the side of the road.

It took my mother more than two hours to trudge, barefoot, along the pitch-black lanes, and she arrived back at the house with her skin red and numbed by the cold. The car was parked in the driveway, the babysitter had gone and my brother and I were asleep in our beds. But, although she searched for him, she could find no sign of my father.

With her teeth chattering and a million tiny needles piercing every inch of her skin, my mother stripped off her soaking wet clothes and wrapped herself in a towel. She knew that she should try to thaw her frozen limbs and raise her body temperature in a warm bath, but she was so miserable and exhausted she couldn't even lift her arms to put on her nightdress. So she just crawled under the bedclothes, and fell instantly asleep.

Just a couple of minutes later, she woke with a start at the sound of the heavy mahogany door of her wardrobe crashing against the wall. Her eyes flew open, but the room was as black as the night and all she could make out was the dark figure of a man leaping out of the wardrobe with a blood-curdling cry. She was so startled and frightened she couldn't breathe, and for a moment she thought she was having a heart attack. She lashed out with her arms and shouted as the man threw himself on top of her, and she continued to struggle with all her might as he pinned her down on the bed, ripped the towel from her shaking body and raped her. And that's when she realised it was my father.

When I saw my mother the next morning, I knew immediately that something really bad had happened. The fact that I lived in constant, unremitting fear of what might be about to occur had made me always alert and watchful, and I could tell as soon as I walked into the kitchen that she was very upset. And, as my mother's distress was only ever due to the things my father did, I knew that he must be in a rage about something and therefore that we were all in danger of feeling the heat of his anger.

Usually, by the time I woke up and went into the kitchen to have my breakfast, my mother was already dressed and carefully made up, her hair shining like the polished shell of a chestnut under the electric light. On that morning, though, she was edging slowly around the room in her dressing-gown and slippers. Her face was pale and her hair uncombed, and when I spoke to her she answered in a flat, dispirited tone and didn't look at me.

I suppose I can understand why my mother fell for my father when they met: he was charismatic and could be affectionate when he wanted to be, and it was easy to imagine him sweeping her off her feet. What *does* seem extraordinary, though, is the fact that she still loved him – which she did. I don't know if he'd ever loved her or whether, for him, it had been a marriage of convenience – her family and background affording him the veneer of respectability that was so important to him, as well as the possibility that she might provide him with access to considerable financial resources. In reality, however, I doubt whether he was capable of feeling genuine love for another person. What he *was* good at was gauging exactly the right moment to be nice to her again so that she was always striving to please him and to win his affection and approval. It was what I did too, as both a child and an adult, and even though there were countless occasions when my father frightened and bullied me, I still just wanted him to like me.

Five

Before Sam was born, I did wonder if all those unhappy memories of my childhood had anything to do with the mild depression I'd begun to feel, and with the 'baby-blues' that developed almost immediately after I took him home from the hospital. I continued to go through the motions of feeding and looking after him, and most of the time I managed to hide – from myself as well as from everyone else – how depressed I was becoming. But when I went back to work, when Sam was 11 weeks old, I began to feel as though I was drowning. I didn't realise I was ill; all I knew was that I was constantly anxious and afraid, and that I'd become incapable of making even the simplest of decisions.

I Remember, Daddy

The house Tom and I had bought when I was pregnant needed a lot doing to it. We knew from the outset that it was going to be a struggle to pay the mortgage – which we could barely afford even on both our incomes – and that I'd have to go back to work as soon as possible after our baby was born. But it seemed worth it to have our own place. We were happy there and when I was pregnant, despite all the fears and worries I had, I'd sometimes stand in the doorway of the room that we were painting and refurbishing as a nursery and allow myself to imagine my baby lying there, safe and warm, in the little wooden cot Tom and I had bought and brought home together so proudly.

For almost as long as I could remember, I'd felt as though I was acting the part of someone leading a normal life – getting a job, falling in love, buying a house and having a baby. Suddenly, though, the role I was playing had expanded beyond anything I had any experience of or could even understand. I was pretending to be someone who was calm and capable, whereas in reality I knew that I was useless and worthless – just as my father had always told me I was – and that I was not at all the sort of person who could look after a baby. There were so many terrible things that could happen to Sam. Many of them were real enough to any first-time mother, but some of them were things I couldn't actually put a name to; and it seemed that

I was the only person who stood between Sam and all those countless, awful, unidentifiable dangers.

I spent every waking moment of every single day in a state of panic. Just the thought of Sam's defenceless little body lying in his cot was enough to make my heart race and the palms of my hands become clammy with sweat. The depression I'd already been suffering from was made worse by the fact that I knew I was supposed to be happy now that I was a mother. And I *did* love Sam, passionately. But, as well as being afraid *for* him, I was also, for some reason, afraid *of* him.

To begin with, no one seemed to notice there was anything wrong. Gradually, though, I could feel myself becoming more detached from Sam and from everything and everyone else in my life. It was as though I was on the outside looking in. I fed him and changed his nappies, but as soon as Tom came home from work I'd almost thrust Sam into his arms. And as soon as I knew that Tom had taken over the responsibility of looking after him, I could finally allow myself to relax a little as I concentrated on what I really wanted to be doing – cleaning the house.

I'd become obsessed by cleaning, to the extent that I eventually found it difficult to think about anything else. Even sitting with Tom watching television in the evenings became a form of torture, and I'd jump up after a few minutes and almost run to the kitchen to scrub the floor or clean a work surface I'd already scoured with bleach half a dozen times that day.

People began to notice how irritable I was becoming, and how often I cried. However, I think even those closest to me had only just begun to realise that something might be wrong, when all the fear and confusion that had been building up inside me finally erupted.

I'd been having terrible nightmares. They'd started at around the time Sam was born and almost all of them involved my father. Night after anxious night, I'd wake up in the middle of a vivid dream, frightened and sweating, with my heart thumping painfully, thinking I was a child again. In some of the dreams, I was hiding in a wardrobe, holding my breath and listening to the slow, heavy tread of footsteps as someone crossed the bedroom floor towards me. I had something draped over my head, so I could only hear the sound of the wardrobe door as it creaked open.

Sometimes, I'd wake up at that point in the dream, waving my arms wildly in front of my face and shouting 'No, no!' And at other times the wardrobe door would swing back on its hinges, the cover would be lifted from my head, and I'd see my father looking down at me. For a moment, I'd feel a sense of relief. But then I'd see that his face was ugly and his expression sneering, and as he reached down and lifted me roughly out of my hiding place, I'd feel a terror so powerful I'd think my heart was going to stop.

On some nights, I'd dream that I was in a bath and I'd stretch out my hand to touch the cool, shiny surface of the blue-tiled wall beside me. Then, suddenly, I'd feel cold and sick, and when I turned my head away from the wall, my father would be sitting in the bath facing me. Dressed in just the jacket of a pinstriped suit, he'd frown angrily at me and say, 'It's your fault, Katie. It's – all – your – fault.'

Sometimes, I'd dream that I was in the bed I used to sleep in as a child and that I'd woken up to find my father leaning over me, completely naked except for a top hat. I'd try to scream, but he'd clamp the short, strong, thick fingers of his hand over my mouth and hiss at me, 'If you say anything, I'll kill you. It won't be the first time I've put someone six feet under.' Then he'd laugh a nasty, humourless laugh, and I'd wake up sobbing.

As the dreams became increasingly frequent, I began to be afraid to go to sleep at all, and before long, as each tiring day was followed by another restless night, I was exhausted.

Then, one morning, a couple of weeks after I'd gone back to work, I stood up from my desk, picked up my jacket and handbag and walked out of the office. As I passed through the reception area, heading for the door to the street, Jackie, the receptionist, called after me, 'Katie! Is anything wrong?' She sounded worried, but I didn't answer her, and I didn't turn around. I didn't want her to see the tears that were pouring down my face and then have to try to explain what it was I was crying about – because I didn't know.

For the next couple of hours, I walked through the streets of the town, wiping my steadily flowing tears on to the sleeve of my jacket, and going nowhere. Eventually, I found myself on a road I recognised; it was the road where Sally lived.

Sally had been my father's girlfriend after my mother left him, when I was seven, and she'd become, briefly, his second wife. She moved into our house just a few days after my mother and I fled into the night, and she slept in my mother's bed and wore the clothes my mother had left behind in her wardrobe.

Despite their apparently similar taste in clothes, though, Sally and my mother were about as different from each other as two people could possibly be. My mother was a neat, house-proud, quietly spoken, well-brought-up, attractive, twinset and pearls sort of woman; whereas Sally was brassy, untidy, chaotic, loudly raucous and hard-headed. But, apparently, my father had been happy to replace a wife who cooked his meals, catered for his parties and looked after his house and children for one whose talents lay in the bedroom.

However, perhaps equally importantly, as far as my father was concerned, was the fact that Sally knew a lot of girls and young women who were willing to go to parties at my father's house and do whatever people wanted them to do in exchange for money. It wasn't long before my father's parties had become legendary, or before alcohol, cocaine and doing exactly what he wanted to do had begun to cloud his better judgement.

My mother had always been timid, and my father had bullied and abused her for so long that she'd eventually lost the ability to defend herself at all. So another way in which Sally differed from my mother was in having a mind of her own, which I think was at least part of the reason why her marriage to my father didn't last. Their split appeared to have been a good deal more amicable than the ending of my parents' marriage, however – which, I used to half-joke, was probably the result of the fact that Sally knew too much about the sexual preferences of my father and of his influential friends for him to have risked making an enemy of her.

Perhaps surprisingly, though, and despite everything, I'd got on quite well with Sally as I got older, and I'd sometimes have a drink with her if I bumped into her in a pub in town. But that didn't explain why I found myself that day standing outside the little house my father had bought for her when they divorced.

Still snivelling pathetically, I rang the doorbell, and then turned immediately and started to walk away.

'Katie! Is that you?' Sally sounded surprised. 'Good God girl, you look awful. Come into the house and hide yourself away till we can sort you out and make you presentable again.'

She stepped forward, placing a hand on each of my shoulders and spinning me round so that she could steer me through the front door and along the hallway into the kitchen.

'You're clearly in need of something a bit stronger than a cup of tea,' she said, opening a cupboard and taking out a bottle of Balvenie Single Malt. She picked up a glass from the draining board beside the dish-filled sink, wiped it briefly on a stained, grey tea towel, and then reached for another. 'Nobody likes to drink on their own,' she added, shrugging her shoulders and smiling as she splashed liberal amounts of whisky into the two glasses. Then she led the way back down the hall and into an elaborately decorated living room that looked as though it had been recently turned over during a burglary.

'Sorry for the mess,' Sally said, tossing piles of magazines off the sofa on to the floor to make space for us to sit down, and not looking sorry at all.

I hadn't uttered a single word since coming into the house. But as I took my first sip of whisky and felt the warmth of it spread down through my chest, it was as though it released something inside me, and the words began tumbling out in a breathless jumble.

'I've been having nightmares,' I told Sally, tears stinging my eyes again. 'They're always about Dad. They're horrible. I don't really understand what's happening in them, but I always wake up feeling frightened and ...' I wiped the back of my hand across my forehead, pushing the damp, matted hair to one side, as I searched for the right word. And then I added, in a voice that didn't sound like mine, 'Dirty.'

Sally had never been one for sentimentality, and her straight-talking, humorously cynical take on life had often made me laugh. So I was surprised to notice that the expression on her face as she looked at me was almost one of sympathetic understanding.

'You don't have to explain,' she told me, swallowing a mouthful of whisky and then taking a long drag on her cigarette. 'I know something happened when you were a child. I know your father did something to you that haunted him in some way.'

'Why? What did he tell you?' I asked. My whole body had started to shake and I felt a mixture of trepidation and anxious excitement at the thought that I was about to hear some revelation that was going to make sense of all the non-sense that had been churning around in my brain for the last few weeks.

'I don't know what's wrong with me,' I told Sally. 'I feel as though there's something terrible hidden just below the surface of my conscious mind. I want to know what it is, but at the same time I'm afraid of it, because I think it's something really bad; something that will affect the way I feel about myself – about everything. Something that proves I'm not a nice person.'

'I don't really know anything,' Sally said, stubbing out her cigarette in a square glass ashtray on the coffee table and immediately lighting another one. 'Except that your father woke up in a cold sweat one night, sobbing like a child and talking what sounded like a lot of gibberish. When I asked him why he was so upset, he said, "Because of what I did to Katie." I didn't know what he meant. He never mentioned it again and I never asked – well, you know your father.'

She looked up at me quickly, and I knew that she was lying – or, at least, that if she didn't actually *know* what my father's nightmare had meant, she had a pretty good idea.

Suddenly, for just a few fleeting moments, all my dreams made sense. I could see clearly in my mind what my father had done to me – and it was far worse than anything I could ever have imagined.

'I know what he meant,' I told Sally.

I watched as the glass fell from my hand – apparently in slow motion – and spattered splashes of whisky across the papers and magazines on the floor beside the coffee table. Then I burst into tears and the picture I had seen in my mind shattered and was gone, leaving me feeling heartbroken and bereft and not understanding the reason why.

I don't remember what happened after that. I think Sally must have phoned Tom and he came to collect me. I found out later that everyone at work had been worried to death when I'd left the office without explanation that morning, and someone had told Tom, who'd been searching for me for a couple of hours before he received Sally's call.

Tom took me home, and his parents came to collect Sam so that he could spend the night with them and I could sleep. But I couldn't get rid of the fear, or of the sound of the voices in my head. I sat on the floor in the corner of the living room for hours, curled into a ball like a child, clutching my knees to my chest and mumbling as I rocked slowly backwards and forwards.

The next morning, Tom rang the doctor's surgery to make an emergency appointment for me, and I told the doctor about the voices, about the terrible fear, and about how I wanted to kill myself because I couldn't bear the flashes of images I kept getting, which were so real and so horrific they almost paralysed me with disgust and self-loathing.

'We need to get you up to the hospital,' the doctor told me. 'Just for an evaluation. Tom can take you.'

He meant a psychiatric evaluation, but I didn't care any more. It was as though there was a person in my head, running in random, chaotic circles of panic, and every time they thought they knew where they were, they found that they were looking down another dark, forbidding corridor to nowhere. I seemed to be outside my body, watching, and unable to do anything to help myself. My whole world had shrunk until nothing existed except a tiny, frightened little girl sitting in a chair, muttering and mumbling to the doctor and trying not to remember.

I allowed Tom to put his arm around my shoulders and lead me out to the car, where I sat beside him in the passenger seat, rocking gently, no longer able or willing to try to reach out and grasp hold of reality.

Tom parked the car in the hospital car park. I don't remember getting out of it, but I must have done so, because I do remember walking with Tom towards a set of double doors that were set in the centre of a large, red-brick Victorian building. Inside, he spoke to someone at the reception desk, who walked with us down an echoing, lino-floored corridor and knocked on one of the many identical grey doors.

The psychiatrist who questioned me gently had grey eyes and darker grey hair, and I remember wondering if greyness was one of the conditions of employment, so that all the people who worked in the hospital would blend in seamlessly with the almost colourless décor. He was kind, though, and he showed none of the irritated impatience I was half-expecting as he explained to me that I would have to be admitted to the hospital while they made a proper assessment of my mental state.

'No.' I spoke the word loudly, with a conviction I didn't really feel. I was no longer sure about anything and I had a terrible, growing feeling that I might be quite mad. But it seemed important not to do or say something that would give anyone else grounds for suspecting there was anything wrong with me. Other-wise, they might lock me up inside this soulless laby-rinth of corridors and ill-health with its smell of floor polish and sickness. And then how would I ever get better?

'No,' I said again, shaking my head as if to empha-sise the determination I was trying to summon up. 'I don't want to stay here. I want to go home.'

'I'm sorry, Katherine. But I'm afraid I'm going to have to insist.' The doctor smiled a small, sympathetic smile. 'Just for a few days, while we sort out what the problem is.'

I stood up, still shaking my head, and he said, 'Please, Katherine. You must stay. I would far rather you agreed to come in voluntarily, because I don't want to section you. But I *will* do so if I have to.'

I'd forgotten Tom was in the room, until I felt his hand on my arm. 'Please, Katie,' he said. 'Just stay here for a couple of days. Let them take care of you until you're feeling well again. Please.'

Suddenly, it was as though someone had pulled out a plug in my body and I could actually see all the energy draining out of me. I seemed to have been struggling to act normally for so long that I'd finally run out of steam and I was too weary and defeated to argue any more.

'Well, okay,' I conceded at last, sitting down heavily in the chair. 'But what about Sam? Who's going to look after Sam if I'm in here?'

'Don't worry about Sam.' Tom's voice was loud with relief. 'My mum and dad and your mum will help me take care of him. You know how much they've been dying to get their hands on him.'

'No one must touch him!' I leapt to my feet and shouted the words in Tom's face. He took a step backwards and I could see the shock and the distress in his eyes. And then, just as quickly as the unidentifiable fear had overwhelmed me, it faded again, and I tried to smile at him as I said, 'Okay. But look after Sam.'

Then I allowed myself to be led from the room and through one locked grey door, down a long grey corridor to another.

Six

I didn't stay in the hospital for just a couple of days, as Tom had thought I would. I stayed there for almost six months, because I was far more ill than he, or anyone else, had realised.

I was put on medication, which eventually quietened, but didn't silence, the clamour of voices in my head, and I was given sleeping tablets every night. I still found it difficult to sleep, though, because although I was frightened all the time, what I was most afraid of were the images I saw when I closed my eyes.

After Sam was born, I'd started to have flashes of half-remembered scenes: being in the bath with my father or lying in bed next to him – or, even more bizarrely, next to one of his friends – and feeling sick.

They were images that had gradually become more detailed, until, by the time I was admitted to the psychiatric hospital, what I was remembering was too horrific for my mind to process it at all.

I hated the hospital. I was terrified of most of the other inmates, particularly the ones who'd suddenly start to shout and try to hurt themselves, or someone else, and who had to be wrestled to the ground by nurses and given injections that turned them – for a while, at least – from ranting, arm-flailing lunatics into limply passive, dead-eyed zombies.

Some of the other patients were suffering from schizophrenia, and they could be the most alarming of all. One moment they'd be talking to you quite normally, and then, suddenly, they'd fly into a rage and accuse you of saying something you hadn't said. You'd stumble away from them, your heart racing with shock, and then you'd begin to wonder if you actually had said it after all. And *that* was even more frightening than the uncontrollable fury you'd just witnessed, because it meant that you never knew what was real and what was in your imagination, or whether perhaps you were crazier than they were.

One day, I was sitting in the day room with a woman who was telling me how much she hated the hospital and the doctors and nurses. She started talking about her family and about how she longed to be at home, and then she suddenly stood up, took a knife from inside the sleeve of her cardigan and tried to slit her throat. I don't know how she'd got hold of the knife, but, fortunately, it was too blunt for her to be able to sever the artery in her neck and kill herself. She made a good attempt, though, and I can remember hearing the sound of what were actually my own wild-animal-like screams as I jumped up from the table, knocking over my chair in my haste to get away from the blood that had started to pour from the wound in her throat.

One of the reasons I was frightened of the other patients was because they weren't like me. And then sometimes I'd be even more afraid because I began to think that perhaps they were, and that I'd be locked up with them for ever. I felt as though I was drowning, looking upwards from just below the surface of the water as I struggled to break through into the air and breathe, but never quite managing to do so.

Because of the medication I was taking, everything seemed blurred and unreal. I felt detached from what was going on around me, as though I'd turned in on myself and was living inside my own head, looking out. I was being dragged back to my childhood because of everything I was remembering and, like a child trying to comfort herself, I'd often sit on the floor in the corner of a room, curled into a ball and rocking backwards and forwards. Sometimes I'd hear the sound of someone crying, and it was only when I stopped rocking for a moment so that I could listen that I realised it was me. Great sobs of despair would rise up from somewhere deep inside me, where they'd been locked away for years. But, no matter how much I cried, I never felt any better.

I'd never forgotten my father's violence towards me when I was a child, and how brutally he used to punish me whenever I did anything 'naughty'. Often over the years, though, when I thought about my childhood, I could almost see something else – something dark and malignant that my mind didn't want to remember. And, while I was in the hospital, those almost-thoughts became memories of the most terrible of all the things my father had done to me when I was a young child – memories that my brain had locked away when I was in my early teens, leaving me with an inexplicable sense of guilt and unhappiness that had underscored every aspect of my life for years.

I'd been desperately unhappy as a teenager; I'd hated my life and I'd hated myself, for reasons I'd never understood. I'd lived with a constant, inexplicable sense of self-disgust and a sometimes overpowering anger that would cause me to lash out and want to hurt people. I didn't know what was wrong with me, and there was no one I could turn to for help. So I'd tried to hide my self-loathing and the turmoil of my emotions beneath a façade of bravado and bad behaviour.

Then, for some reason, the birth of my child had triggered the unlocking of some of those previously repressed memories. At first, they were just flashes of unfocused images; but, gradually, they became complete pictures that I didn't want to look at but that I could no longer ignore. And, eventually, my brain had blown a fuse and I'd become so mentally disorientated and so uncertain of what was real and what I was imagining that my mind had been unable to process any thoughts or function on any level at all, which was when I'd ended up in hospital.

Luckily, though, I had a wonderful psychiatrist. Dr Hendriks was the first person I'd ever talked to about the things I was remembering, and I was reluctant to talk about them at all to begin with, not least because it was almost impossible to find the words to describe the images I was seeing. But Dr Hendriks always listened without judging me and, perhaps most importantly of all, he made it clear that not only did he believe what I was telling him, but that he didn't blame me for what had happened to me as a child. Because, as well as beginning to remember what my father used to do to me, and what he allowed and encouraged his friends to do too, I remembered that he had always told me that all of it was my fault – and the responsibility of that belief was a burden I'd carried throughout my life.

I'd been at the hospital for just a few days when I walked out of the day room one morning and heard a commotion at the end of the corridor. There were often quarrels and scuffles of one sort or another – patients fighting amongst themselves or arguing with the nurses – and I'd quickly learned to be wary and alert to the signs that indicated something was kicking off. So, without looking overtly in the direction from which the noise was coming, I stopped and listened.

In every door along the corridor there was a small window, but it was only the one in the door at the end that looked out on to the normal, unlocked world outside. I glanced quickly towards it and could see part of what appeared to be an enormous bunch of flowers. On *my* side of the door – the locked, crazy side – there were two nurses. The smaller one of the two was on tiptoes, looking out through the window, while the other one stood at right-angles to her, glancing back down the corridor in my direction.

As soon as the second nurse saw me standing nervously in the doorway of the day room, she scurried towards me.

'Go back, Katie,' she said, looking directly into my face and nodding a couple of times, as if to encourage me to do what she was asking. 'Go back in the day room. Please. It's just for a moment.'

There was an urgency in her voice that made the muscles of my stomach contract, and I stepped quickly back into the room. The nurse closed the door behind me and I stood for a moment, my whole body shaking violently, and tried to breathe. Then I turned to look through the little window in the door. But all I could see were the neat brown curls at the back of the nurse's head. So, instead of looking, I listened, one ear pressed against the wired glass.

I could hear the subdued murmur of a woman's voice, which was interrupted periodically by a man saying something loud and angry. For a few seconds, everything was quiet, and then a different man spoke in a slow, authoritative voice. The first man shouted, a door slammed and then there was silence.

My heart was racing and, as I took a step away from the day-room door, I could see the damp imprint of my hand where it had been pressed against the glass of the window. At that moment, the nurse turned and smiled at me and then she opened the door.

'Well done, love,' she said. 'You can pop out now.'

'Who was it?' I whispered. 'Who was the man who was shouting?' But I already knew the answer.

'It was your father,' the nurse said. She smiled a quick, apologetic smile.

Usually, the staff avoided any kind of physical contact with the patients, except when they had to restrain someone who had become violent and was threatening to hurt themselves or someone else. For some reason, though, the nurse touched my arm lightly as she added, 'My word! Now there's a man who knows what he wants and intends to get it.'

I pressed my hands against my stomach, trying to stop the sick feeling rising up into my throat, and then I asked, in a barely audible voice, 'And what *did* he want?'

'Oh, he wanted to see you. In fact, he *demanded* to see you. Apparently, he's on the hospital board.' Her laugh was scornful.

My father told me the same thing himself some years later, which is when I found out that it wasn't true. He wasn't on the board of hospital directors, as he claimed to the nurses that day, although I've no doubt he knew people who were. But twisting the truth – and telling outright lies – to get what he wanted was something he often did, and he must have been furious when his self-assured, bullying arrogance hadn't had its usual effect and he'd been thwarted in his attempt to see me.

The other man's voice I'd heard during the fracas with my father turned out to have been that of Dr Hendriks.

'How dare you try to prevent me from visiting my daughter,' my father had bellowed at him. 'I demand to see her immediately.'

'I'm afraid that won't be possible, and I must ask you to leave – now,' Dr Hendriks had answered. He always spoke in calm, measured tones, which I found reassuring, but they must have driven my father into a frenzy of fury – particularly in view of the fact that Dr Hendriks was someone my father would have referred to as 'a bloody foreigner'.

I couldn't begin to imagine how enraged my father must have been at being refused access to me, not to mention at being spoken to as if he was 'just anybody'. He'd have heard on the grapevine that I was remembering things about my childhood, and he must have been anxious to find out what I was saying. I expect he wasn't too worried, though, because, after all, who was going to believe the word of a crazy woman who'd been committed to a psychiatric hospital against that of a successful businessman, friend to the rich and famous, and well-known pillar of society? My breakdown must have seemed like a godsend to him.

After my father had stomped out of the hospital in a rage that day, a nurse handed me the huge, stupid bouquet of flowers he'd left for me. I rammed them into the bin, heads first, snapping their stems and scattering their petals on the floor around me.

I'd always been frightened of my father. Just thinking about him made the hairs on the back of my neck stand up and my stomach start to churn painfully. But, for a moment, that fear had been replaced by hatred, and I felt a deep, childish satisfaction at the thought that, for once, he hadn't got his own way. I was grateful to the nurses and to Dr Hendriks for standing up to him in a way I'd never seen anyone do before, and for making me feel, briefly, safer.

A few days later, Sally came to see me. I was surprised by her visit, not least because I was certain that sick-visiting of any sort wasn't something she'd normally do. We sat together at a grey, plastic-topped table in the dreary, smoked-filled day room and she offered me a cigarette. A nurse was sitting in a low armchair in a corner of the room, reading a newspaper, and she glanced up occasionally to look at Sally with ill-disguised distaste. The bright, gaudy colour of Sally's scooped-neck T-shirt and her carefully applied make-up were in stark contrast to the drabness of everything around her, and I noticed the openly interested stares of the other patients in the room, as well as the shock in Sally's eyes as she saw how grubby, dishevelled and unkempt I'd become.

I was happy to have her there, though, if only because it meant that I could ask her the question I whispered repeatedly to everyone: 'Can you get me out of here? I need to go home. There's nothing wrong with me. Please, can you get me out?' And Sally answered it as everyone did, by telling me that I was there for my own good and that I'd soon be better and at home again. Then she sat smoking her cigarette and making circles with her finger in the spilt water on the table, while I rambled incoherently.

Suddenly, she interrupted me, glancing up at me quickly and then looking away again as she said, 'What is it that you're remembering, Katie? What *sort* of things?'

I launched into an explanation that was really just a tangle of disconnected words, and she began to look impatient. I'd seen the same expression in the eyes of everyone who came to visit people at the hospital – a mixture of sympathy, distress and an almost palpable longing to be anywhere else in the world but where they were.

She interrupted me again, forcing herself to smile encouragingly as she asked, 'Can you give me an example of something you've remembered?'

At that moment, the nurse stood up, folded her newspaper and said, 'I think that's enough excitement for one day, don't you Katie?' Then she turned to Sally and added, in a briskly terse tone, 'I'm afraid I'm going to have to ask you to leave now.'

Sally stubbed out her cigarette. Then she leaned across the table, patted my hand and sighed as she said, 'Goodbye, Katie. Take care of yourself.'

She stopped for a moment in the doorway, turning to look at me with a rueful smile, and then she left.

It was only later that I realised the only reason she'd come to see me was because my father had sent her. Having been unable to gain access to me himself, he'd told her to come and grill me about what I was remembering and what I was telling the doctor. Looking back on it now, I'm glad he did that, because it meant he was afraid. But, at the time, I was too ill to gain much satisfaction from anything and too traumatised by all the things I was remembering even to think about how those memories might affect my father.

When I was in the hospital, I spent a lot of time re-living my childhood. I'd often sit on the floor in the corner of my room, partially protected by the walls on either side of me, and talk in a high-pitched, child's voice about the things I was afraid of. I was remembering just some of the unspeakable things my father had done to me from the time I was three years old, and some of the disgusting, appalling things he'd made me do to him, and my mind simply couldn't cope. I felt contaminated by my childhood, dirty and repulsive; and, despite the medication I was taking, I became intent on killing myself, because I couldn't bear the thought of having to live with the guilt and with the knowledge of what I thought *I* had done.

For years, I'd suppressed all the memories that were starting to return. So when I was a teenager and everything had seemed so inexplicably miserable, I hadn't understood what was wrong with me and why I didn't seem to fit the life I was living. Sometimes when I was young, sudden waves of rage would wash over me. I knew they were out of all proportion to whatever had just happened, but it was as though I couldn't help myself and I'd be completely overcome by the need to lash out and hurt someone. It was a rage that had often frightened me and that had made me as wary and distrustful of *myself* as I always was of anyone I didn't know well. Perhaps what had been one of the most difficult things of all, though, was the knowledge that I wasn't the person I wanted to be, or even the person I felt I really *was*, somewhere deep down inside.

In hospital, as the memories started to re-surface – and with Dr Hendriks's help – I began to understand what had caused all those years of unhappiness when I'd seemed constantly to have been fighting an invisible enemy. And, in some ways, remembering was almost worse than not knowing.

When my mother came to see me, I could tell she was trying to sound optimistic, as though she truly believed I'd get better and would be able to live a normal life again. She'd never known about most of the things I was remembering, and I didn't tell her about them until some time later. So I suppose she couldn't understand what had happened to make me so ill. On more than one occasion, I heard her say to one of the nurses, 'Katie shouldn't be in here with all these people with schizophrenia – and worse. She's not like them. She's not mentally ill.'

She was wrong, though. I was regularly regressing to childhood, re-living its nightmares over and over again, and I was hearing voices telling me that I was useless and dirty and that I might as well be dead. And the reality was that I was about as 'mental' as it was possible to be.

I'd never had much of an appetite, even as a child, and in hospital I almost stopped eating entirely and began to lose weight. Starving myself was just another form of the self-harming I'd been doing even before I went into the hospital, when I'd often cut my arms to try to release some of the pain that had built up inside me.

Whenever I was allowed out of the locked ward to go for a walk with a nurse, I'd keep my eyes fixed to the ground and, as soon as she looked the other way, I'd stoop quickly to pick up anything sharp I could see. Sometimes, I'd find a tiny shard of glass and sometimes I'd snatch up a nail that had been kicked into the gutter beside the pavement. I'd slip it into a pocket or up inside my sleeve and hide it in my room until I was alone and could take it out and cut myself. Then I'd watch the blood trickle down the soft skin on the inner surface of my arm towards my wrist, imagining that it was a red line of pain washing out of my body. And it worked, a bit, for a while.

I was always trying to think of ways to escape from the hospital. I'd spend hours standing beside the locked door to the outside world, murmuring to myself and trying to look nonchalant as I waited for someone to be let in or out of the ward so that I could make a dash for freedom. Surprisingly, I did manage to get out once or twice, although I can't now remember how.

One day, someone found me wandering along the side of the road not far from the hospital, and on another occasion I made it all the way to a friend's house. I don't know how I got there, but I remember asking her over and over again to promise she wouldn't tell anyone, because if they made me go back to the hospital, I knew I'd die. She did promise eventually, and then she phoned Tom when I was in the bathroom and he came to pick me up. I was furious with my friend and I was convinced that, like everyone else, she was part of a cruel conspiracy to keep me locked up when there was nothing wrong with me.

'I'll never speak to you again,' I shouted at her. 'I thought you were my friend. I thought I could trust you. I can't believe you've done this to me.'

She cried as she tried to explain her reasons for doing what she'd done. 'You're not well, Katie,' she told me. 'And if you don't go back to the hospital, you might never be well again. I *have* to do what I think is right. So either you let Tom take you back, or I'll call the police and you can go back with them.'

I hated her for a while, but she was right. I was very ill, and the truth was that if I couldn't cope in hospital, where the doctors and nurses were trying to help me, then I'd never be able to cope in the 'normal world' outside.

After a while, I was put on lithium, a powerful drug that's used to treat psychosis; and as the medication began to have an effect, I was moved to the hospital's mother and baby ward, where Sam was allowed to stay with me. For weeks, I don't think I'd been consciously aware of anything other than my own fears and memories. So it felt good to be able to hold Sam and to think that perhaps, one day, I'd lead a normal life and be a proper mother to him.

At first, Sam stayed with me just for the occasional night, then for a weekend and then, for the last few weeks before I went home, he was with me all the time. I understood that everyone had to be absolutely certain I'd be able to manage and look after him on my own, and I went through the motions and did all the things I was supposed to do, although I didn't really believe I'd ever be able to look after anyone or anything – including myself.

There were still some days when I relapsed into a world where nothing made sense except fear. And, on one of them, when Tom came to visit, he found me wandering in the hospital car park, half-naked, murmuring to myself and holding Sam tightly in my arms. I don't remember how I'd got out of the locked ward, but I *can* still recall Tom's obvious anxiety and the tears I could see in his eyes, and how miserable and guilty I felt at the thought that I'd made him sad.

Gradually, though, I began to get better and, after I'd been in hospital for six months, I was allowed to go home. In reality, however, 'better' is a relative term, because I still needed a lot of support – from Tom, his family and social services – and I wasn't well enough to go back to work.

On Christmas Day, about three months after I'd come out of hospital, Tom suggested we should accept my father's invitation to 'pop in' and have a drink with him and his girlfriend, Gillian. We'd had our house for just over a year by that time, but we were struggling financially and couldn't pay the mortgage, and Tom was carrying all the stress and worry of it alone. So it seemed remarkable to me that, despite my illness and everything else he'd had to deal with over the last few months, he wanted to see my father so that he could ask his permission to marry me.

I desperately *didn't* want to see my father. Tom knew that he'd been physically violent towards me when I was a child, but, as I hadn't talked to anyone except my psychiatrist about the things I was remembering, it was difficult to think of a reason that might explain why I was so reluctant to visit him on that occasion. So we went to his house in the afternoon.

By the time we arrived, my father was in the jovial stage of drunkenness. It was the first time he'd seen his grandson and as he held Sam out at arm's length and said something jokily critical about him, I looked at his face and felt suddenly ill.

'I have to get out of here,' I whispered to Tom. 'I'm going to be sick. I'm sorry but I need to leave – right now.'

'What on earth's the matter?' Tom asked me. 'You look terrible.'

I could see the nervous anxiety in his eyes and I knew he was afraid that I was breaking down again.

'Please, let's just go,' I said, pushing Sam's things into a bag and then reaching out to snatch my son from my father's arms.

I Remember, Daddy

'What? Leaving so soon?' My father's tone was mocking. 'But you've only just got here. Oh well, why don't you take some champagne for your mother? There are some steaks in the kitchen, too. Perhaps she'd like some of those.'

He waved his arm in a magnanimous, lord-of-the-manor sort of way as he spoke, and I felt a wave of disgusted resentment and a determination not to accept his pathetic handouts for my mother.

I shook my head and he shrugged and then suddenly bellowed at me, in a voice you might use to address someone who was partially deaf and feeble-minded, 'You all better now? Not mental any more?'

Gillian gasped and I felt Tom's body stiffen beside me. But my father just laughed.

'You were on lithium I hear.' He looked directly into my eyes for the first time since we'd arrived, and then he turned towards Gillian as he said, 'When nothing else works for psychotics, they bring out the big guns. Then you *know* you're dealing with a real nutcase.'

Gillian's face was scarlet with embarrassment and distress. But my father just turned his head to look at me again and said slowly, 'And who's ever going to believe the word of someone like that?'

Tom took a step towards him, but I put my hand on his arm as I said, 'Please, let's just leave.' Then I walked ahead of him out of the room.

My father had threatened me before, and I knew exactly what he was saying: whatever happened in the future and whatever I might say about him, I was now a once-certified mad woman – and he felt safe in the knowledge that no one would ever take my word against his.

Seven

I hadn't understood the flashes of images I was seeing before and after I was admitted to hospital. They seemed to be of dislocated scenes, which, although they didn't make sense, always left me feeling deeply disturbed and distressed. And I think that if I hadn't gradually learned to trust Dr Hendriks and been able to talk to him about what I was remembering, I might never have come out at the other end of the dark, terrifying tunnel I seemed to be in.

The trouble was, though, that once the floodgates had opened, there was no way of controlling the flow of memories that were being released.

Extraordinary as it seems now, despite what I was remembering about the things my father used to do to me, part of me continued to want him to love me. I simply couldn't make any sense of *why* he'd hurt me and abused me and not loved me, and I thought it was my fault. I'd accepted for years that I was responsible for anything bad that happened to me or to the people I cared for, because that's what my father had always told me. So it was difficult to override that 'reality' and replace it with the knowledge that I wasn't to blame for what had been done to me when I was a child. And it was only two or three years ago when I finally realised that my father's love was something I neither needed nor desired.

One of the first clear memories I had when I was in the hospital was of something that happened when I was three years old. It seemed random and didn't make much sense to begin with, until I realised that it was just one piece of the jigsaw that I was starting to put together, with Dr Hendriks's help.

The memory was of a time when I was very young and my father's parents were staying with us. They were sitting in the kitchen one morning, drinking their early-morning cups of tea, when I appeared in the doorway in my nightdress and told them I had a really bad itch.

'Well, that won't do now, will it?' my grandfather said, lifting me on to his lap and kissing the top of my head.

I Remember, Daddy

I loved my grandfather. He was always kind and patient with me, and he told the most wonderful stories, which was something my father must have inherited from him – together, sadly, with his alcoholism.

'And where is this terrible itch?' my grandfather asked, sliding me down his legs on to the floor and then pulling me up by the arms so that I was sitting on his knee again.

I laughed delightedly, and then pointed to my 'front bottom' as I said, 'It's down there.'

I started to lift my nightdress, but my grandmother reached out her hand to stop me, saying firmly, 'There's no need to show us, dear. I expect it's just irritation caused by soap or washing powder. I'll tell Mummy to make sure she's rinsing your clothes properly and then I'm sure it'll go away. Just don't scratch it.'

Nothing more was ever said to me about it, even when, shortly afterwards, I developed a rash of boils on the same area of my body. At first, they were just small, itchy, red spots. But they quickly grew larger and more painful, until they were so bad I could hardly walk and the doctor had to come to the house to lance them. Even then, no one seemed to wonder *why* a three-year-old child had boils around her genitalia. These days, I imagine, questions would be asked. But, in the 1960s, I doubt whether anyone ever considered the possibility of sexual abuse within a family – and certainly not in a family like ours, with a father who was a high-earning, well-connected and well-respected businessman.

I used to wonder what my mother thought had caused those boils. But she was naïve, and as used to feeling responsible for bad things as I was to become, so she probably remained convinced that she'd caused them by not rinsing the washing powder out of my clothes properly.

In many of my childhood memories, my mother isn't present. Even when she was at home, she'd usually be in the kitchen, two floors below the rooms where my brother and I spent most of our time as children, while we were looked after by whoever was our current nanny. We had a constantly changing stream of nannies – who were actually au pairs rather than qualified child carers, as that name would suggest. None of them lasted very long, because my father slept with all of them and when my mother found out, she got rid of them, one by one. However, a casual observer might not have noticed when one left and another took her place, as it was difficult to distinguish between all the young, blonde, pretty Scandinavian girls my father insisted on employing. There was one, though, that I remember clearly. She was different from all the others, being English and dark-haired, but everyone agreed that she adored me. Her name was Margaret Kennedy.

One day, just after Sam was born, I found a photograph of myself, aged about three, wearing a pretty pink dress and standing barefoot in a garden I didn't recognise. I asked my mother where it had been taken and whose garden it was.

'It was at Margaret Kennedy's house,' she told me. She took the photo from my hands and smiled. 'She loved you so much. She and your father used to take you there sometimes, so that she could show you off to her family and friends.'

I suddenly felt as though I was going to be sick. I closed my eyes and kept swallowing the saliva that was flooding into my mouth until eventually the feeling passed and I reached out and took the photograph from my mother's hand. I examined the photo for a moment and then looked at my mother. Even for someone who'd been too brainwashed and under my father's thumb to think about it at the time, I was certain that she must have realised how ridiculous what she'd just said had sounded and be wondering why my father had gone with Margaret on those visits to her home. But apparently not, because she was still smiling wistfully at some fond memory of my childhood the photograph had falsely evoked.

Suddenly, an image flashed into my mind: I was lying on a bed and Margaret was holding my arms above my head, pressing them against the mattress until they hurt. Then, as quickly as it had come, the picture evaporated and was gone, leaving me feeling as though someone had punched me in the stomach and dreading the prospect of remembering whatever had happened next.

The photograph I'd looked at with my mother that day represented just one of the causes of the many hours I spent crying and rocking myself backwards and forwards in the corner of my room at the hospital. Because the memory it had begun to unlock was of what really happened when my father and Margaret Kennedy were together.

Although my father had simply slept with all my other nannies, he'd had a more serious affair with Margaret. And she didn't take me to her house to 'show me off' to other people, as she always claimed; she took me there so that my father could sexually abuse me while she held me down on the bed.

As all our other nannies had done, Margaret had a room on the top floor of our house, which she stayed in during the week, and she and my father often used to take me there, too. I didn't have even the slightest understanding of what my father was doing to me at the time; all I knew was that I hated it. But I didn't cry, partly because what he did to me when Margaret was there wasn't as bad as being thrashed with his belt. It did hurt, though, and it made me feel miserable, because it was like being punished for something and because it sometimes seemed as though my father didn't even really know I was there at all.

Once I started to remember, and the images I could see in my mind developed from fragments into full memories, it was too late to decide that I didn't want to know. Sometimes, I'd remember something and have an almost triumphant sense of 'I knew it!,' because part of me had always known there must be a reason why I felt so unhappy and so 'unclean'. Most of the time, though, I wished I wasn't remembering, because being forced to relive my childhood seemed far worse than not knowing what had happened to me. But I *had* to remember. I had to face the demons that were scrambling my brain and making me so ill, because only by doing so could I take the first step on the long, exhausting and often incredibly difficult journey towards recovery.

I was just three years old the first time my father had full intercourse with me. He came into my room one night when I was asleep and climbed into bed beside me. Not long after that, I started lining up all my dolls next to my pillow every night, in the hope that when my father came silently into my room, he wouldn't be able to tell which little head was mine. When that failed, I began sleeping in a corner of my wardrobe with a sheet draped over my head – which was one of the first images that had haunted my nightmares after Sam was born. But, again, my father wasn't fooled, and almost every night the wardrobe door would slowly creak open and he'd reach in to lift me out and carry me back to my bed before lying down beside me.

Sometimes, he'd put a pillow over my face while he abused me and, just once, he called me 'Mother'. Mostly, though, he seemed to be in a trance. He wasn't nice to me while he was doing it, but he wasn't horrible, and I think that, for as long as he was breathing loud, rasping breaths and making peculiar grunting sounds, he was completely unaware of who I was.

My father didn't really *do* anything other than work, drink and sleep. Every Saturday, he'd go out to meet friends for lunch. Then he'd come home, drunk, in the afternoon and say casually to my mother, 'I'm going upstairs to have a nap. I'll take Katie with me,' or – the sentence I dreaded more than anything else – 'Katie might as well come with me while I have a bath.'

No one talked openly about anything in those days, including domestic violence and sexual abuse, and my mother was probably even less worldly wise than most people of her background and upbringing. So she never had even the slightest suspicion about what my father was really doing to me – and I'm not sure what she'd have done if she had. I'd like to think she'd have taken some sort of action to put an end to it. But my father had already broken whatever spirit she used to have and she'd long ago given up arguing with him about anything, because she'd learned that all that would happen was that he'd beat her up and then do whatever it was he'd been planning to do in the first place.

So, when my father took me upstairs with him, she'd just feel pleased that at least he was taking some interest in me. Then she'd go down to the kitchen and start preparing food for the evening's party.

In the bedroom, my father would tell me to take off my clothes and get into the bed, and then he'd make me tickle him or show me the special way he liked to be massaged. After a while, he'd take hold of my hand, place it on his penis and say, 'Now look what you've done! It's your fault that's happened, so you're going to have to get rid of it.' Then he'd half-lie on top of me, crushing me with his weight and hurting me as he heaved and grunted. And I'd feel bad, because I knew that I was to blame, even though I didn't understand what he was doing or why.

Afterwards, he'd fall into a deep, alcohol-fuelled sleep, and I'd lie beside him, watching the saliva dribbling from his open mouth and the sides of his nostrils vibrating in time with the rumbling of his snores. When he woke up, he'd give me a pound note – later, a shiny new one-pound coin – which was a small fortune to me at the time.

Far worse than being taken into my father's bed, though, was having to have a bath with him. I was frightened of my father, and I'd learned at a very young age that it was best to do whatever he told me to do, promptly and without fuss. So when he pushed my head under the water and held it there, I tried not to panic or to think about the pain in my chest as the air drained out of my lungs, because I knew that the quicker I did what he'd taught me to do, the sooner I'd be able to breathe again.

I didn't know there was anything wrong with what my father was doing to me or with what he was making me do to him, any more than I'd have thought it might be 'wrong' of him to teach me to recite fables in French. I just accepted it; in fact, I didn't really even think about it. If I had, though, I imagine I'd have assumed that all fathers did the same things to their daughters; that all daughters were to blame for what was done to them, as my father always told me I was; and that all little girls hated it as much as I did. I didn't have friends home to tea, and I rarely went to anyone else's house to play. So I didn't know that other fathers didn't punch their wives and abuse their children, or that not every little girl had an empty space inside her that was slowly filling up with hurt, fear and self-hatred.

My father drank in bars and pubs at lunchtime almost every day, including weekends. He'd often arrive home late on Friday afternoons with at least one friend, and they'd have a few drinks together before going out again in the evening. One Friday afternoon when I was four years old, I went into the kitchen and found my father leaning against the black iron range cooker drinking a glass of whisky and talking to his friend Harvey Wynne.

Harvey Wynne had extraordinarily bushy eyebrows and a long, narrow chin, which made him look far more serious than he actually was. He was always nice to me, and as I walked into the kitchen, he greeted me cheerily.

'Well, hello there, Miss Katie,' he said in a jokey, cartoon sort of voice. 'That's a very pretty dress you're wearing today.'

He smiled broadly at me, and then picked up a crystal whisky glass from the kitchen table and raised it to his lips.

'It's a new dress,' I told him proudly. 'My mummy bought it for me when she went shopping today.'

'Well, it suits you very well,' Harvey Wynne said, sitting down abruptly and heavily in one of the oak-wood chairs beside the kitchen table. He turned to look at my father, who smiled and nodded, and then he patted his knee as he said, 'Why don't you come and sit here, with your Uncle Harvey.'

I was always afraid of doing anything that might make my father angry with me, and I glanced up at him quickly to see if he approved, and again he nodded his head. So I climbed on to Harvey Wynne's knee in my lovely new dress, and he let me dip my finger in his whisky and laughed when I wrinkled my nose with disgust at the taste. Then he put his hand underneath the skirt of my pretty dress, pushed it down into my pants and touched me with his fingers, while my father looked on, sipping his drink and smiling a small, cold smile that warned me not to struggle and cry out, as I wanted to do.

After a while, my father told me to 'run along', and as I slid off Harvey Wynne's knee, he handed me a shiny coin and I left the room clutching it so tightly that my fingernails dug painfully into my palm, leaving tiny red marks like half-moons. But, despite my delight at being given this token of my father's apparent approval, I couldn't help feeling that something really bad had just happened.

Shortly after that day, my father went on a holiday to Spain with some of his friends. They'd rented a villa for a couple of weeks, but he'd only been there for a few days when he got ill and he summoned my mother to fly out and look after him. My brother had been at boarding school since the age of five, but it was the school holidays, so my mother had to take us both with her.

I remember how excited I was at the thought of going on an aeroplane, although I don't remember much about the days we spent at the villa in Spain, except that I had to run as fast as I could across the burning hot sand to the water's edge when we went to the beach, and that we ate delicious, thick omelettes that tasted far better than anything I'd ever eaten at home. And I remember swimming one day in the pool at the villa with one of my father's friends.

For some reason, we were the only two people at the pool that morning and he was supposed to be keeping an eye on me while I was in the water. I was wearing bright-orange-coloured water wings on my arms and splashing around happily just out of my depth when he swam towards me, pulled the bottom of my swimming costume to one side and put his penis inside me. It hurt and startled me, and when I screamed he quickly took it out again, stared at me coldly as he splashed me with water and then swam away.

Back at home, my father's parties had become legendary, and sometimes, after I'd gone to bed at night, I'd creep out of my room again and crouch silently in my nightdress on the landing, so that I could look down through the balusters. I loved hearing the laughter and listening to the loud, cheerful chatter of my father's jovial friends, which was often punctuated by shrieks from the confidently mini-skirted, flirting young women they'd brought with them. My father and his friends seemed to know a lot of young women, and it wasn't until later that I realised they'd actually picked them up in casinos and bars because they were willing to have sex with almost anyone in exchange for as much of my father's expensive champagne as they could drink.

After most of the parties, at least one of my father's friends would be too drunk to go home, so he'd stay the night in a guestroom on the top floor of our house. And on those nights, from the time I was just four years old, my father would come into my bedroom when I was fast asleep, pull back the bedclothes and lift me out of my bed. Sometimes, I'd open my eyes as he was carrying me up the stairs, and sometimes I'd wake up to find myself already lying in a bed beside some man I didn't know who was breathing alcohol into my face and touching me.

Whenever I saw any of my father's friends during the day, they'd speak pleasantly to me and I'd answer them politely. At night, though, when I lay naked in bed beside them, they rarely said anything directly to me. They all stank of alcohol, and one of them – my father's best friend, who was later accused of abusing his own stepdaughter – had feet which smelt so awful that just being in bed beside him made me retch.

But although I hated what was happening and it made me afraid to fall asleep at night, none of the men who abused me was actually *unkind* to me in any practical way that I could identify. So I simply assumed it was what everyone did – that it was just one of those things you had to accept when you were a little girl and no one was interested in what you wanted or what you thought. It was many years before I had any understanding of what was normal behaviour towards a child and what was totally unacceptable, perverted and cruel abuse. Until then, I was just happy when someone was kind to me.

It was no wonder I'd fallen apart after my own child was born. In my mind, being a child was associated with being constantly unhappy, bullied and frightened and, subconsciously, with sexual abuse. The prospect of becoming a parent had scared me before Sam was born, and the responsibility of knowing that I had to protect him against all the dangers I could name, as well as those I couldn't, had proved overwhelming. And, gradually, while I was in hospital, I began to understand why.

Eight

As a child, not knowing what was 'normal' and what wasn't meant that I trusted everyone and no one, and that I had no basis on which to judge people's intentions. There was one occasion, when I was five, when I was playing outside in the street and a man stopped in his car and asked if he could take my photograph. Nowadays, no normal person would even consider making a request of that sort to a little girl playing on her own. But perhaps at that time people were more trusting, or simply more naïve. So I sat down on a step outside the house, as he asked me to do, and he took my photo and promised to send me a copy.

When I proudly told my mother what had happened, she was horrified. The colour drained out of her face and she bent down, put her hands on my shoulders and looked directly into my eyes as she said, 'Oh Katie! Surely you know that you mustn't, ever, talk to strangers. I can't believe you let a strange man take a photo of you.'

'But he wasn't strange,' I told her, wondering if perhaps my understanding of the word was different from my mother's. Then, feeling pleased with myself for being able to clinch the argument so definitively, I added, 'His feet didn't smell.'

My mother just looked at me in bewilderment and shook her head. Unable to follow what to me seemed like a logical train of thought, she must have wondered if I was simple, at best.

Several days later, there was a knock on the front door and when my mother opened it, a man thrust what looked like a piece of paper towards her.

'I took this photograph of your daughter a couple of weeks ago,' he told her. 'I hope that was okay. She was playing in the street outside and although she looked like a little ragamuffin, you could tell she'd been immaculately clean and tidy when she'd first gone out. I thought she was the most beautiful child I'd ever seen.'

My mother was mollified – she still has the photograph to this day – and she was vastly relieved to discover that the man I'd told her about wasn't the devil she'd thought he must be. Which was ironic really, because she hadn't any idea that it wasn't 'strange men' on the street I needed to be wary and afraid of; it was my own father and the men she regularly talked to and laughed with and entertained in her own house.

My father's abuse continued almost every night for more than four years, until being miserable seemed normal and I was becoming increasingly confused about what was right and what was wrong. And then, in the middle of one night when I was seven years old and he was out with his friends, my mother came into my bedroom, woke me up and told me to get dressed.

I pulled the bedcovers over my head and turned away from her. But she knelt down on the floor beside my bed and pushed at my shoulder until I eventually rolled over with a sigh. When I looked at her, I saw that her eyes were red and full of tears and I knew something very serious was wrong.

'Get up, Katie,' she whispered, tugging at my arm. 'We've got to go. Get dressed, quickly. Here, I'll help you.'

She picked up a sweater from the chair beside my bed and as she fumbled to pull it over my head, she raised her arms and the sleeves of her blouse slipped back to reveal skin that was almost completely covered in black and yellow marks.

I Remember, Daddy

'We *must* go before your father gets home,' she said, in a voice full of fear and urgency. Then she turned and started pulling clothes out of my drawers and stuffing them into an already over-full suitcase, glancing over her shoulder towards the bedroom door every few seconds as though she expected my father to walk through it at any minute.

She was more frightened than I'd ever seen her before, and my heart began to beat so fast I thought it might suddenly wear itself out and stop, because I knew she was right to be afraid. It was my own constant fear that one day my father might punch or kick her so hard that he'd kill her without meaning to, and I knew that if he came home and found her in the process of leaving him, he'd be so angry that this could be the night when my worst nightmare came true.

It was term time, so my brother was at boarding school, which meant that it was just me and my mother who crept, hand in hand, down the stairs that night and fled from the house without a backward glance. My mother had taken nothing with her except the few clothes she'd flung hastily into a suitcase and then dragged down the stone steps on to the pavement, and I don't think I really believed we were leaving for good.

We spent the rest of that night at the house of one of my mother's friends, and the next day we drove in almost unbroken silence to her parents' house, where she was going to leave me while she went to London to look for work.

I still couldn't believe we'd escaped from my father – or that anyone *could* escape from him – and for weeks I kept expecting him to appear suddenly in front of me and tell me that he was taking me home. But the truth probably was that he was pleased to be rid of us; he was always telling us how 'fucking useless and pathetic' we were and how we were too stupid to follow even the simplest of instructions. Despite our glaringly irrefutable inadequacies, however, he must have been beside himself with rage when he discovered that my mother had dared to take the initiative and leave him. He certainly wasn't heartbroken, though, because, just a few days after we'd gone, he moved his girlfriend, Sally, into the house.

For my father, who loved sex, parties and drinking above all else, Sally was the ideal partner. She wasn't a good housekeeper like my mother, though. My mother had always been house-proud and conscientious about making sure that everything was spotlessly clean, which was how my father always insisted it should be. So, when I visited him some time later, I was shocked at how untidy the house had become. There was mess everywhere. Almost every flat surface in the living room was covered in dirty glasses and plates with the congealed remains of food stuck to them; and there were more stacked up in the sink in the kitchen. Clearly, Sally's other skills outweighed her obvious lack of interest in housekeeping.

My father went through a wild phase while he was with Sally. Although he'd never really seemed to care what people thought about him – despite the fact that, paradoxically, other people's opinions of him were exactly what drove his long-held need to *be* someone – he'd always managed to keep up a front of respectability. But, when he was with Sally, he started taking cocaine and drinking even more heavily than he'd done before, and sex became the focus of his life.

Meanwhile, I lived with my grandparents, while my mother rented a flat in London. She didn't really settle there, though. It was a long way from where she'd grown up, and from her friends and family, and marriage to my father had left her too cowed and lacking in confidence to be able to strike out on her own and make a success of a completely new life.

I wasn't happy either. I was a very odd little girl and people generally didn't like me. I didn't understand why and, unfortunately, no one explained to me what it was that I did wrong – even when the father of a little girl at school came to my grandparents' house one day and angrily told my grandfather that I was not to play with or even talk to his daughter ever again.

Katie Matthews

I longed to have friends, but there were so many confusions and conflicts in my mind, and my behaviour was so strange, that I made people wary and uncomfortable around me. And the more unhappy and isolated I became, the more I did things that highlighted the difference between me and all the other children at school.

From the age of seven, I'd sometimes take money from my grandmother's purse and buy cigarettes from a cigarette machine. I don't know why I did it – needless to say, none of the other children at school smoked. Perhaps it was a way of expressing the sense of freedom I felt when my father was no longer controlling my every move, because I knew that of all the many things my father hated, he hated people smoking almost worst of all. Or perhaps it was a case of 'might as well be hung for a sheep as a lamb': if I was going to be stuck with a reputation for being 'odd', I might as well be as odd as it was possible for me to be.

My mother stayed in London for almost a year, and then one day she came to collect me from my grandparents' house. I think they were vastly relieved to see me go, and I was certainly happy to be returning with my mother to the city where I'd been born, even though the prospect of seeing my father again filled me with dread.

I Remember, Daddy

For the first few weeks, my mother and I stayed with a friend of hers called Tilly, who had a flat on the first floor of a house similar to – and not far away from – the one we'd lived in with my father. One night while we were there, I was woken up by the sound of someone shouting in the street below my bedroom window. Still half asleep, I'd turned on to my back to listen when suddenly my eyes snapped open and I was fully awake. It felt as though ice-cold water was flooding through every vein in my body, because I recognised the voice that was shouting in the street outside: it was my father.

With my heart thumping, I slid out of bed, crept to the window and then just stood there, trying to pluck up the courage to look out on to the street. Eventually, I took a deep breath and lifted the edge of the heavy velvet curtain. I could see my father standing on the pavement outside the house, waving his arms in the air like someone conducting an invisible orchestra and shouting words I couldn't make out. I dropped the curtain quickly, as though I'd been burned, and crawled back under the blankets on my bed, where I lay, crying soundlessly, until I fell asleep.

The next morning, it was Tilly who opened her bedroom curtains first and saw the photographs my father had rammed down on to every single one of the spikes on the black-painted iron railings that ran across the front of the house. My mother cried when she saw the torn, scarred photographs of her wedding to my father and, although it seemed totally inexplicable to me, it was obvious that she still loved him, on some level at least, and that she was deeply hurt by what he'd done. She was distraught, too, when she found out that his girlfriend Sally had given away her wedding dress and had been wearing the clothes she'd had to leave behind in her wardrobe the night we fled from our home.

Clearly, my father was intent on making my mother suffer for having left him.

My mother no longer had any money of her own and, despite the divorce settlement ordered by the courts, my father gave her nothing. He had an almost psychopathic hatred of anyone who crossed him and he had always had absolutely no interest in 'doing the right thing'. All that ever concerned him was what *he* wanted – and he wanted money almost more than anything else. So he simply ignored the court order, assuming – rightly, as it turned out – that my mother wouldn't have the mental energy to fight him and that if she ever did, he had enough powerful and influential friends in high places to find some way of discrediting any claim she might make.

My father had been hiding money for some time and he'd bought several properties, most of them in the names of trusted friends. So he allowed my mother and me to move into a flat in a house he owned, for which, incongruously, my mother paid him rent. It was a horrible flat – just two rooms plus a tiny kitchen and an even tinier bathroom in a rundown house in one of the worst areas of town. I had never seen anything like it before, and in fact I didn't have any idea that places like that even existed.

My father was in the process of having the rest of the house divided up into dismal little bedsits, and for the first few weeks after we moved in, we were its only occupants. The whole building was grimly bleak. It was noisy during the day when the workmen were there and eerie at night while all the bedsits were empty. But, once our new neighbours started moving in – all of them drunks, drug addicts and prostitutes whose rents were being paid by social services – it was worse than anything I could ever have imagined.

Our flat was on the top floor, and it was divided from the landing at the top of the staircase by a glass partition, which meant that our hallway – and the doors leading off it to the bedroom, bathroom, kitchen and living room – was clearly visible to anyone and everyone coming and going to the bedsits.

I think my father derived some sort of satisfaction from knowing that my mother was living in such a miserable place – and I know that he was completely indifferent to what happened to me. Perhaps he felt that living surrounded by down-and-outs and criminals was suitable punishment for her for having thought she could just walk away from him. And perhaps he liked the irony of the fact that my mother had come from a respectable, comfortably well-off family whereas he had been poor as a child, and now *she* was living in squalid poverty while *he* remained in the family home, dined at the best restaurants and drank champagne with some of the town's most prominent movers and shakers.

Every corner of the flat was pervaded by a sour, musty smell, which no amount of scrubbing and cleaning could ever get rid of. There was no washing machine, no cooker and no furniture apart from the narrow single bed I slept in and the sofa in the living room, which at night became my mother's bed. The bathroom was minute; it was too small for a bath, and there was just a grimy, leaking shower with no curtain rail, and therefore no curtain, a cracked basin and a stained toilet with a white plastic seat that jerked precariously to one side when you sat on it. There was no floor covering in the bathroom; in fact, there were no curtains or floor coverings anywhere in the flat, except for two large Persian rugs my mother had somehow managed to take from what was now my father's house and which looked bizarrely out of place on the stained, splintered floorboards in the living room/bedroom.

My mother's mother bought us a cooker, but we still had no washing machine, so we washed our clothes in the basin in the bathroom and hung them to dry on a rack in the shower.

My mother found a job in an upmarket clothes shop, where she earned just enough to pay the rent and bills, and I accepted things as they were, without ever thinking that there might be an alternative way for us to live. I realise now that my mother must have been depressed, and still completely under my father's thumb. Why else would someone who wasn't receiving the money from her ex-husband that the courts had ordered him to pay actually pay *him* money for rent on a horrible, disgusting flat like the one we were living in – or, in fact, for any flat at all?

Although my parents had always done a lot of socialising and my mother had occasionally come home from a dinner or a party slightly tipsy, she'd never been a heavy drinker like my father. After we moved into the flat, though, she began to drink much more, and she'd often farm me out to stay with other people. I'd sometimes spend weeks at friends' houses, sharing the normal lives they lived with fathers who were kind and reasonable and didn't fly into rages and beat them or their mothers and who didn't creep into their bedrooms at night or prostitute them out to their friends.

Those were the best weeks of my life at that time, although, in some ways, they came too late, because the seeds of my own depression had already been sown and I think my mind had already begun to block out the worst and most distressing of my childhood memories – the unravelling of which after my son was born was to make me so ill that it came close to destroying me.

My mother would often rant and rave about my father, particularly when she'd had too much to drink. But she'd still let him in whenever he came to the flat, and I'd be sent out on some stupid errand and told not to come back for two hours. I knew what they were doing – or, at least, that they were doing 'it'. And when I got back to the flat, after wandering miserably around streets that no reasonable adult would take a child to at all, my father would have gone and my mother would be giggly and girlish for a while, before sinking once again into a state of listless crying.

One evening, before the work in the house had been completed and my mother and I were still the only tenants, there was a knock at the front door of the flat and I opened it to find my father standing there, one hand resting on the door jamb. He was drunk, although apparently not yet at the aggressive stage of drunkenness, and he pushed me aside as he walked into the hallway and said, 'Where's your mother?'

'She's in there,' I told him, pointing towards the living room. Then I went back into my bedroom and closed the door.

The walls of the flat were made of flimsy plasterboard, and I could hear the murmur of my parents' voices, although I couldn't make out what they were saying. And then I heard my father shout, 'You *will* bloody sign it, woman. Just do it.'

'But it's *my* house. It's the only thing I've got left,' my mother said, in the whining voice that had always irritated my father.

The palms of my hands began to sweat.

'Sign it!' my father screamed.

I heard a thud and then my mother shouted, 'Help, Katie! Get the police.'

It was in the days before everyone had mobile phones, and there was no telephone in the flat. It was dark outside and the nearest call-box was several streets away. I was nervous about walking through our neighbourhood in broad daylight, and I never left the flat on my own at night. But I knew that on this occasion there was no alternative and that I had to go.

I tried not to make a sound as I eased open my bedroom door. But I'd taken just one step into the hallway when my father burst out of the living room and bellowed at me, 'If you go, she'll be dead when you get back.'

I just stood there, paralysed by fear and indecision, and then my father reached out his hand, grabbed me by the hair and dragged me into the living room.

'Just sit there and watch,' he shouted, pushing me towards a corner of the room and forcing me down until I was crouching on the rough floorboards.

He turned towards my mother, who curled up on the sofa with her arms over her head as she tried to protect herself against the punches and kicks he rained down on her from above.

On the many occasions while they were married when my father had attacked my mother, he'd always been careful to avoid marking her face, or any other part of her body where the bruises would be visible. This time, however, he didn't seem to care, and blood was already pouring out of her nose and from a huge gash above her eye.

I sat on the floor where my father had thrown me, hugging my knees against my chest and whimpering. I'd always been afraid that one day he'd go too far and I was certain that, this time, my mother was going to die. A voice in my head kept repeating the words my father had so often shouted at me – 'You're useless. You're nothing but a worthless piece of shit' – and I hated myself for not having the courage to make a dash for the door and then run out into the street and try to get help. But, quite apart from the fact that I was so frightened I didn't think I could force myself to move at all, I knew that if I did stand up, my father would simply kill me too.

Suddenly, he reached out his hand towards the little table by the sofa, snatched up a heavy glass ashtray and brought it crashing down on my mother's head. I started to scream hysterically as blood spattered across the sofa and on to the wall behind it and my mother's limp body fell back against the cushions. I was still screaming when my father yanked me by the arms, pulling me roughly to my feet, and shouted into my face, 'Stop that bloody noise and come with me.'

He dragged me down the hallway and into the bathroom, where he turned on the taps and began to run water into the cracked washbasin, leaving a trail of blood over everything he touched.

'Wash them,' he told me, lowering his stained, blood-soaked hands into the water. And I obeyed him, because, unable to process the horror of having witnessed my own mother die at the hands of my father, my mind had shut down and I was no longer capable of thinking at all.

My father dried his hands on the thin blue towel that hung on a half-attached rail beside the shower, and then he pushed me ahead of him back into the living room.

I didn't want to see my mother's body, but I knew I couldn't just pretend that nothing had happened. So I shut my eyes, took a deep breath and then opened them again and looked quickly towards the sofa. My mother's head was resting at an unnatural angle against a cushion and the top half of her body was soaked in blood. I began to sob.

'For Christ's sake, shut up,' my father hissed, pushing past me as he walked towards the sofa and then leaned down to pull my mother up by the arms into a sitting position. As he moved her, a thin, barely audible moaning sound escaped from her lips and then her eyes flicked open and she reached up her hand to touch her head.

I wanted to throw my arms around her and hug her, but I was too afraid to move. Instead, I stood completely still and watched as her eyelids closed again and she slumped back against the arm of the sofa. Again, my father pulled her up, more roughly this time, and propped her into a sitting position with some of the blood-stained cushions from the sofa. Then he turned, straightened a piece of paper on the little table, took a pen from the inside pocket of his jacket, unscrewed its cap and put it into my mother's hand, folding his fingers tightly around hers as he said, 'Now! Sign it.'

I Remember, Daddy

Still slipping in and out of consciousness, my mother signed over to my father her one remaining possession – the house by the coast, which he planned to sell so that he could pay off some of his gambling debts. Then he put the lid back on his pen, placed the pen carefully in his pocket, blew briefly on my mother's wet signature, folded the paper and left, without a backward glance.

As the door of the flat slammed shut behind my father, my mother sank back on to the sofa and appeared to stop breathing.

'Don't die, Mummy,' I pleaded in a whisper, standing beside her but not daring to touch her thin, fragile, blood-drenched body. 'Please, Mummy. Please don't die.'

She moved her lips, but no sound came out of them and I bent down towards her so that I could put my ear close to her mouth.

'Get Eileen,' she murmured.

Eileen was a friend of my mother's, a sensible, down-to-earth woman who never allowed her emotions to overrule her commonsense. I felt almost sick with relief at the thought that Eileen would know exactly what to do. And this time I did find the courage to run out into the dark streets to the phone box.

When Eileen arrived, she'd already phoned for an ambulance and my mother was taken to hospital, where incredulous doctors shrugged resignedly as she insisted she'd fallen and banged her head.

Even after my father had come so close to killing her, he'd still occasionally turn up at the flat and my mother would let him in. Sometimes, he'd search every room, looking for any signs that a man had been staying there. I never understood why my mother put up with it, but they had very complicated feelings about each other. Although they appeared to hate each other – with good reason on my mother's part – each of them was jealous at the thought that the other one might have other relationships, even though my father was with Sally at the time. My father had nothing to be jealous of, though, because my mother had no man in her life. So they kept doing what she called 'getting back together', although it rarely lasted longer than one night, at most, and on my father's side it had nothing to do with anything other than sex and control.

I'd sometimes visit my father and stay overnight with him. I didn't want to see him at all, but he told my mother that, if necessary, he'd get a court order to enforce regular 'visitation rights'. So she told me that it would be better if I went of my own accord, because that way I wouldn't have to go every week.

Sometimes when I went to see my father, Sally would be there. But they often had huge rows, which resulted in her slamming out of the house and staying away for a few days, and then I'd have to sleep in his bed with him. He was drinking very heavily at that time, as well as taking cocaine, and he was still throwing extravagant parties, at which he sometimes made me dance for his friends.

However, the real focus of the parties was sex. Most of the women who went to them were young – some of them only in their mid-teens – and a lot of them were working prostitutes. The men were almost all highly paid, well-respected professional men who were friends and colleagues of my father. Some of them were well known, either locally or, in some cases, nationally, and most of them would have had a great deal to lose if people had been aware of how they spent their leisure time. The only people who did know about it, though, were the girls – who were well paid to keep their mouths shut – and other men who were doing the same thing. So they all felt safe in the knowledge that no one was going to dish the dirt on them.

For many of them – including my father – the power that came with their professional positions had made them arrogant and they believed that they were beyond and above the law. If nemesis ever threatened my father, however, he knew that all he had to do was let it be known that he had in his possession some very interesting and explicit photographs of people who might not want their private lives to be made public.

In some ways, my life didn't really improve after my mother left my father. Although for most of the time I was free of his bullying cruelty and the terrible anxiety that resulted from living every day under his tyrannical control, I still had to visit him and sleep in his bed when Sally wasn't there. And, on the nights when I stayed with him, I was still lifted out of my bed in my sleep and placed in a bed beside his friends. Sometimes, they touched me and sometimes they had sex with someone else while I lay there miserably, my eyes tightly shut as I tried to imagine I was anywhere in the world except where I really was. Sometimes, I'd see a flash and – as I got a bit older and began to understand what was happening – I'd feel deeply ashamed at the thought that my humiliating degradation had been immortalised in a photograph.

From being a bit of a misfit at the age of seven, when my mother left my father, I became over the next couple of years a very odd little girl indeed.

For as long as I could remember, I'd had all sorts of obsessions – things like 'If I don't reach that lamppost before that car gets to the zebra crossing, something terrible is going to happen to me.' And I only ate when I was forced to; by the time I was ten, I weighed less than 4 stone. I realise now that it was a form of self-harming, but at the time no one seemed to wonder *why* I was trying to starve myself to death.

I Remember, Daddy

Perhaps my mother just assumed it was because I'd spent the first seven years of my life being bullied, both physically and mentally, by a cruel, aggressive father. She did take me to the doctor, though, when I was on the verge of becoming anorexic, and he gave me some disgusting green, gloopy stuff to drink every day. It was supposed to make me hungry and to provide me with some calories and nutrition. But it tasted so revolting that drinking it seemed like a punishment in itself.

Despite everything, though, I did have friends at school, although I never really trusted anyone and I felt as though no one knew the real me. But I wasn't a nice little girl.

I was afraid that if I allowed anyone to get close to me, they'd discover I was an imposter, because I was really a horrible, useless person, just like my father always said I was, who was tainted in some way I didn't understand. And because there was no one I could talk to about my thoughts and fears, I created some imaginary friends – Clarence Groon and his wife, also called Clarence Groon, and their Clarence Groon babies.

The Clarence Groons were balls of fluff, which I'd hold up against my face in my cupped hands while I whispered to them about all the things I could never have told anyone else. In fact, they were *imaginary* balls of fluff – my cupped hands were empty – and I think my mother was a bit spooked by it all.

She used to ask me repeatedly why I was always talking to them and what I was saying. Oddly, though, I think she was more impatient with me than concerned about why I might need to have imaginary friends to talk to – particularly, perhaps, such peculiar, non-living ones. In my mind, though, the Clarence Groons were real friends I could trust, and I told them everything, including my darkest, bleakest thoughts.

I used to fantasise about my death, even at that young age, and I'd often do mad, sometimes danger-ous, things. For example, one day when I was out with a friend, I jumped, fully clothed, off the high bank beside a waterfall, hurling myself into the cascading, foaming water and falling with it into the pool below. My friend was frantic. I could hear her screams as I jumped, and when she came running and stumbling down the rocks to the pool, I think she expected to find me lying there dead. By the time she reached me, however, I was climbing out of the water, bruised but otherwise not seriously hurt, although, even so, she was so shocked that she never really forgave me. She was convinced that I was crazy – and perhaps she was right.

There was a ball of tightly wound anger inside me, which sometimes burst out so that I lost my temper without warning. On one occasion, I grabbed hold of a girl who was talking to me and shoved her head between some railings, and someone had to call the fire brigade to get her out. No one could understand why I'd done it and I didn't even try to explain. But the truth was that she was a girl who used to bully me. She'd made my life a misery for a long time, and I'd done nothing about it. Until, on that day, she'd said something that had annoyed me and I'd suddenly felt a red-hot rage flooding through me, and all I could think about was getting my own back on her for all the hurt and humiliation I'd suffered at her hands.

After incidents like that, I'd have no memory of what I'd done. It was as though I'd had a black-out, and when someone told me about it, I wouldn't believe them and I'd say, 'No, I didn't do that. No, that wasn't me.' Because deep down inside I knew that I wasn't someone who behaved in that way; it just wasn't who I was. I can understand now what was happening and why there was so much suppressed fury inside me. But, at the time, there didn't seem to be any rational explanation for it, and I began to worry that there was something seriously wrong with me.

Nine

I hated the world I was living in as a child; so I created a whole new fantasy world that I could retreat to whenever I was unhappy – which, for years, was almost all of the time. I'd read books about kings and queens and imagine I was living in *their* world, and I was forever finding little things and hiding them away, pretending to myself that they were priceless treasures.

One day, when my parents were still married and I was very young, I'd been visiting my father's parents when my grandfather told me about a ring he'd lost in his garden shed. Every time I went to stay with them after that, I searched for it and, some years later, I told my grandfather, 'I still haven't found that ring you lost, Granddad. But I promise I won't give up looking.'

I Remember, Daddy

My grandfather seemed bemused. 'What ring?' he asked. 'I don't know what you're talking about, Katie.'

'The ring you lost in the shed,' I said. 'I still look for it every time I come here.'

He stared at me for a moment and then, as understanding dawned, said, 'But Katie, I made that up. There never was any ring. I just told you that to give you something to do that day. I thought you realised.'

I was devastated. Not only was there no treasure to be found in the shed, but I'd spent hours searching for something that didn't exist. I'd often imagined the look of delight my grandfather would have on his face when finally, triumphantly, I handed him his precious long-lost ring, and I'd never given up believing that one day I *would* find it for him.

I probably trusted my grandfather more than anyone, and I was completely shocked to realise he'd lied to me. And, in that moment, I had a premonition that everything I had ever believed in or hoped for was going to turn out to be just as empty and pointless.

I can only remember one period when I was happy as a child. It was a long summer holiday when I was ten and my brother and I went to stay with my father's parents in a house by the sea. It was an unusually hot summer and we woke up every morning for weeks to brilliant sunshine and clear blue skies. On most days, we went fishing with my grandfather; then we picked raspberries and made jam with my grandmother; and in the evenings, after dinner, we all played cards together.

Normally, no one ever did things like that with us. At home, it had always been clear that my father's preference was for us to be seen when required and not heard at all. I honestly don't think it would ever have crossed his mind, at any stage during my childhood, to have played a game with me – at least, not any game that it was intended for children to play.

I'd never before felt so free and at ease with myself as I did during those days spent with my grandparents that summer. And they remained, far and away, the best days of my entire childhood.

My grandmother was a tiny, fiery, God-fearing despot who left no one in any doubt about the fact that she ruled the roost. When I was very young, she used to read to me from the Bible, and although it wasn't *all* fire and brimstone and eternal damnation, she certainly took the Ten Commandments very seriously indeed. Everyone was terrified of her, including my grandfather. But I loved her. My grandfather was my favourite, though – in fact, he was probably the person I loved best in the world. He was a lovely, gentle man who was really interested in people.

My father's parents weren't at all like my mother's parents, who were old-school strict and who slapped me if I was naughty. Although my father's father was an alcoholic, he was always good tempered. Sadly, he died the year after that summer holiday, and I rarely saw my grandmother again after that. My father had always been her favourite child, but when my parents split up and he got together with Sally and started to lead an openly wild life, my grandmother refused to have anything to do with him.

Years later, I visited my grandmother and found her alone in a cold, soulless high-rise flat, cooking on an open fire. I left her some money and then phoned my father to tell him how his mother was living.

'I can't do anything,' he told me. 'I haven't got any money myself.'

It was a ludicrous claim, although one he often made.

He may have heard my snort of derision, because, after a moment's silence, he said, 'Well, I'll see what I can do. I'll send her something and make sure she's all right.'

He told me later that he'd been sending her money every week since that phone call, but I discovered that in fact he'd never sent her a single penny.

She died a few years ago, and he didn't go to her funeral – choosing, instead, to send a 'representative', who was someone she'd never even met. He did, however, make a magnanimous donation to the nursing home where she'd spent her final years – and where he'd never visited her – with instructions that the money was to be used to buy a brand new state-of-the-art wheelchair. The people at the nursing home must have thought he was a very strange man indeed.

For me, one of the best things about spending time with my grandparents that summer had been that they'd made me feel like a normal child; whereas, for the rest of my childhood, I never felt as though I fitted in anywhere, and I didn't know why. I'd often watch and listen to other children, trying to work out what it was okay to do and say. But, however hard I tried, the world just didn't make sense to me. I was never certain about anything, and I seemed always to be in a state of bewildered confusion.

When I was 11, my mother and I moved out of the flat my father had rented out to us, when, one day, out of the blue, he said we had to leave. I can't remember the excuse he gave my mother, but I found out later that it was because he wanted to sell the building to raise money to pay off some of his gambling debts – again. So we packed up our bits of stuff and left that horrible bleak flat and went to live in a slightly larger two-bedroom place in a marginally better area of town.

The new flat was at the top of a long road where, someone told me, there'd once been a gruesome murder. I had a friend who lived at the other end of the road, and whenever I walked to her house, I'd be in such a state of nervous anxiety I could barely breathe. I'd glance continuously from side to side and over my shoulder, longing to break into a run, but terrified in case doing so drew the attention of the murderer, who, I was sure, was still there somewhere, watching from a window in one of the blank-faced houses.

One day, I was walking along the road with my friend on the way to her house when a car pulled up beside us. The driver wound down his window and said something I couldn't hear and then he beckoned me over. My friend hung back, but I stepped across the pavement towards the car. The man rested his arm through the open window and as I looked down I saw that his other hand was holding his penis and that he appeared to be totally naked from the waist down.

I screamed and tried to jump back, away from the car, but he grabbed my arm, his fingernails digging painfully into my skin. My friend ran off down the road, crying in loud, breathless sobs, and the man started to get out of his car, still gripping my arm tightly. I tried to pull away, tugging and twisting my wrist, and then suddenly I was free. I shouted to my friend as I ran down the road after her, and we both darted together through an open gateway that led to a tennis club.

Although there were people playing tennis and others coming and going between the building and the tennis courts, I didn't even think to tell anyone what had just happened. Instead, my friend and I watched from behind the fence as the man drove slowly down the road, did a U-turn and drove slowly past us again. Then, as he was turning the car around for a second time, we clasped hands and ran together out of the tennis-club gate and down the road to my friend's house, where her mother phoned the police.

When the police arrived, we told them what had happened, but the man was never caught. My friend's mother – and, later, my own – expressed dismay that I'd approached the man's car in the way I had, and both mothers reminded me again about never talking to strangers I didn't know. Their warnings and advice served little purpose, though, other than to increase my already high level of anxiety and confusion about what sort of men doing what sort of things one needed to be wary of.

I didn't often visit my father at that time. I used to tell my mother I didn't want to stay overnight with him at all, although I never explained why. Ever since I'd been able to understand words, he'd told me repeatedly that I was worthless, useless, a little scrubber who'd end up in care because nobody loved me. And I had no reason not to believe him. I don't think he ever told me in so many words not to talk about what he did to me, but I didn't, partly because he managed to make me feel as though it was my fault and because he'd often tell me that I was a slut, 'Just like your mother'.

My mother was never a slut, though; she was a lady, whose only real crime was not having the self-confidence and strength of character to stand up to my father until it was too late, both for her and for me. The way my father treated her while they were married, and afterwards, completely destroyed her sense of assurance and self-worth, and she never fully recovered from the hurt he inflicted on her, both physically and, more importantly, mentally.

I don't suppose I'll ever fully recover from what he did to me either. I believe that what happens to a child during the first few years of its life becomes the foundation for its understanding of everything. And, by his actions, my father ensured that the foundations of *my* life were a sense of worthlessness and a longing to be loved that were to colour everything I did and everything that happened to me for years, and that I still have to struggle against on an almost daily basis. I kept trying to please him and trying to gain his approval – whether by reciting fables in French without error or by being a 'good girl' and lying still when he took me into his bed and abused me in a way that still haunts my nightmares.

Occasionally, when he and his girlfriend, Sally, had a row, instead of storming out herself, she'd kick him out of the house – which was something that seemed completely amazing to me, as I couldn't imagine anyone ever having the guts to do that. And it was on one of those occasions, when I was 12 years old – not long after the incident with the masturbating man in the car – that my father sexually abused me for the last time.

After Sally had locked him out, he'd gone to stay with his friend Angus, who'd moved into a flat in a nice part of town, and one night when I was staying there with him, they had a party. I was annoyed at having to be there at all, because although Angus was being nice to me, as he always was, my father clearly didn't want to be bothered with me. I'd retreated huffily to the bedroom where I slept with my father whenever I stayed there with him and was reading my book when he came in and said, 'Get out there and entertain everyone.'

I instantly felt sick. The whole flat was vibrating to the sound of the music that was blaring out from the stereo. I knew that everyone was already drunk and that most of them had taken drugs, and I dreaded the thought of having to stand in front of them and dance, which was what my father wanted me to do. But I was still as terrified of him as I'd always been, and it never crossed my mind not to do what he told me to do. If I entertained his friends, he'd be pleased with me; if I didn't, he'd be angry, and when he was angry he hurt and frightened me.

I put down my book, took a deep breath and went into the living room, where I began to dance. Afterwards, my father took me into a bedroom and told me to take my clothes off and get into the bed. I waited anxiously for whatever was about to happen, and after a few minutes the door opened and a man I didn't recognise came in, followed by a younger woman. Neither of them spoke to me as they took off their clothes, climbed into the bed beside me and started having sex, and I lay there silently with tears of humiliation and shame trickling slowly down my cheeks.

Later, my father took me to his bedroom and abused me, and that's where I woke up beside him the next morning.

I didn't see him very often after that, except when he wanted some information about my mother or when he decided to remind me that he was still in control.

Even when I was very young, there were many days when everything seemed so hopeless and miserable that I wanted to kill myself. The people who knew me were used to my sometimes odd behaviour, so I don't suppose I seemed any different to them on those days from the way I did on any others. However, by the time I was in my early teens, it had become clear to my mother that there was something wrong with me. She had her own problems, though, and although she had some discussions with my father – and I think also with someone at my school – about the possibility of sending me to see a psychiatrist, nothing ever came of it, and I was left to carry on trying to battle my demons on my own.

My mother was working during the week and she used to go out quite a lot at the weekends, so she was never really around very much, and perhaps she didn't realise just how unhappy I really was. She says she loves me very much, and I'm sure that's true; but, as a teenager particularly, I was difficult and moody and she must have been glad when I went to stay with friends – sometimes for weeks on end – and left her free to do her own thing.

During my first year at secondary school, I stayed with my friend Megan and her parents for more than 140 days, during which time I went to see my mum just twice. I loved living with Megan in her comfortable home, rather than in our grotty flat. I loved being able to lie in the bath in a warm, nicely decorated bathroom and then walk barefoot across the thick carpet on the landing to the bedroom, where I could draw the flower-patterned curtains and shut out the night.

I Remember, Daddy

I'm still very close to Megan. She says now that I was like a poor lost soul, and I think that's the way I felt, although I wasn't really conscious of it at the time. It just seemed as though I had nothing to live for. I desperately wanted to be 'normal', but something set me apart from all the other girls I knew, something indefinable that I was deeply ashamed of and didn't understand.

I rarely visited my father when I was in my teens. When I did do so, there were always young girls hanging around the house drinking. Some of them were girls who went to my school and were just two or three years older than me, and my father – who was in his mid- to late forties – was sleeping with at least one of them, who was 15 years old. He used to show me a photo album that was full of pictures of young girls posing topless; and there was often a porn film showing on the TV when I arrived at his house.

As his gambling debts increased, he and Sally ended up living on just the bottom floor of the house, while he converted all the floors above into flats, which he let out to friends who were either single men or in the process of divorce. And I was employed – at the age of 12 – to clean for them. It was my father's friend Angus who suggested it. He was a wheeler-dealer and apparently a very hard man in his day, although to me he was always just Uncle Angus, who tried to look after me in any way he could. He'd gone to live in one of my father's flats when he separated from his wife, and he was sharing it with another man, an antiquarian bookseller whose 'thing' was having sex with under-age boys.

Angus gave me a key to the flat and I'd go there when they were out, at weekends and in the school holidays, to clean, wash the dishes and change the sheets on the beds. Like all the other flats in the house, it was a disgusting, filthy mess. But, even at the age of 12, I felt as though I'd seen it all and nothing could really faze me.

One day, my father told me he was going to have a party and he asked if I and a couple of my friends wanted to be waitresses. He gave us £20 each – which was a great deal of money to us at the time – and a few days later we arrived at his house and awaited our instructions.

For a couple of hours, we handed round drinks, smiling politely at the increasingly inappropriate comments made to us by my father's lecherous friends and giggling together in the kitchen. Then, when everyone was already well on the way to being drunk, my father walked into the centre of the living room, pulling Sally with him, tapped his glass a few times to get everyone's attention, and announced their engagement.

I Remember, Daddy

I hadn't known anything about it and I was furious. It felt as though my father had tricked me into being there, to make it seem like I was okay with the idea of him marrying Sally. But I wasn't okay with it, not least because I knew that – for reasons that didn't make any sense to me – my mother would be devastated.

Whenever he had a party, my father used to fill the bath with ice and expensive bottles of champagne, and while everyone was still congratulating the happy couple, my two friends and I snuck into the bathroom, popped all the corks and then left the house. It felt good to have got my revenge on my father, although I don't know if he ever realised how it had happened, because he was already drunk when the party started.

Not long afterwards, he and Sally were married in a beautiful Victorian Gothic church that was almost overflowing with wedding guests. Sally wore a white dress and walked slowly up the aisle beneath the soaring stone ceiling, flanked on either side by rows of smartly dressed local dignitaries – many of whom regularly attended my father's parties – and their unsuspecting wives.

My mother didn't want me to go to the wedding, but my father insisted and, for some reason I never understood, I cried the whole way through the ceremony. Then everyone piled out of the church and drove to an exclusive hotel, where they ate elaborately prepared and presented food, got drunk on costly champagne and acted as though the marriage of the wealthy businessman with whose young daughter some of them had shared a bed was an occurrence worthy of the heartiest congratulations.

Shortly after the wedding, my father sold the house that had been our family home and moved with Sally to a large detached house in the suburbs. There didn't seem to be any point in going to visit him there. He was never affectionate towards me, and whenever I did see him he moaned and complained about my mother. But sometimes he insisted, although it was clear that he didn't have any interest in being a father. We never did normal father/daughter things together, because everything was about him and what he wanted.

He did take me shopping one day, though. It was during one of the periods after my parents divorced when they were talking to each other and my mother had somehow managed to persuade him to buy me an outfit I desperately wanted, but that she couldn't afford. I can remember counting the days until the Saturday and then running along behind my father as he strode to the store. I showed him the clothes I wanted and he took one look, laughed and walked away. I felt humiliated and embarrassed and so disap- pointed I had to bite the inside of my cheeks to prevent myself bursting into tears in the middle of the shop.

I Remember, Daddy

My father looked smugly satisfied, as though he'd done something clever, and when I didn't answer him when he spoke to me, he accused me irritably of being sullen and ungrateful – although, as he'd bought me nothing, I couldn't for the life of me think what I was supposed to be grateful for.

I trailed miserably after him to all the shops he wanted to go to, and then we met up with his friend Angus, who must have seen how disappointed I was and felt sorry for me, because he bought me a pair of shoes and some boots and ignored my father's shoulder-shrugging sneers.

I had very little contact with my brother throughout my childhood. He was away at boarding school during term time, and in the holidays he stayed with friends or with my father. I knew my mother loved us both, but that she loved my brother most and that seeing him so rarely made her miserable. She continued to drink at the weekends, sometimes quite heavily, and when she was drunk she'd cry and say, 'I worked so hard to bring you and your brother up and now my life is terrible. Your father is so awful to me, after everything I've done for him ...'

To me, they seemed to be tirades of self-pitying justification, and I dreaded them. I hated myself and I hated my life, and I had very little sympathy for anyone else's misery, perhaps particularly my mother's. As soon as she started to moan, I'd interrupt her by saying, 'For God's sake get your act together,' and she'd look at me reproachfully and take another sip of her drink.

Then, one day, she met someone and her life was transformed almost overnight.

My mother was in her forties and Paul was at least 15 years younger than she was. But he had a good job and he treated her really well. I felt pleased for her, because it seemed that she'd finally found a purpose to her life. She stopped drinking and gained a confidence that I didn't remember ever seeing in her before, and after a while Paul moved in to live with us.

He was kind to me and he made it clear that he knew how I might feel about having someone else living in the flat I was used to sharing with just my mother. I liked him, though, and I could see what a difference he was making to my mother's life. So I was almost as happy to have him there as she was.

Then, one morning, he went to work as usual and never came back. My mother was devastated. It was as though someone had flicked a switch that had turned off the light he'd lit inside her. You could actually see the hurt in her eyes, and I didn't know what to say to her. So I took the coward's way out and tried to avoid saying anything at all. I don't know why I was surprised about what had happened, because I'd already learned

that everything ends in tears and that even when someone appears to love you and care about you, they really
don't. But that wasn't something I was able to talk
about with my mother.

She didn't see or hear from Paul again until she
bumped into him one day in town, years later. She
asked him what had happened, what she'd done that
had made him walk out on her when things seemed to
be going so well between them. And he told her that
his friends had teased him about their relationship,
and had kept saying, 'Just imagine when she's 50 and
you're only ... Or when she's 60 and you're ...'

He'd hated their constant jibes and had eventually
allowed them to convince him that his relationship
with my mother would never work out. He'd known
how heartbroken she would be, how she'd lose all the
confidence she'd gained from feeling that he loved her,
and he hadn't been able to find the words to tell her.
So he'd said nothing at all.

I don't think my mother ever really recovered from
the hurt she felt about what Paul had done, and
although she had other boyfriends after him, she never
let anyone get so close to her again.

It was a feeling I understood, and I shared my
mother's reluctance to trust anyone. By the age of 12,
with just one happy memory – of the summer holiday
I'd spent with my grandparents – I was on the verge of

becoming a deeply unhappy teenager. I'd already suppressed the memories of the sexual abuse I'd suffered at the hands of my father and his friends. So I was left with an immutable, deeply rooted feeling that I was different from all the other girls I knew, and that I was unlovable, for reasons I didn't understand.

When I did something odd – which happened often – people used to say, 'Oh, you're mad!' And I really thought I was. I had suicidal thoughts every single day and I can remember one day when I was 12 feeling such a profound sense of despair that I looked out of the window of the flat I lived in with my mother and thought, 'I could just finish it now. All I have to do is open the window and jump.'

But it seemed as though I was too useless even to do that.

Ten

I was a horrible teenager. I drank and smoked and had an anger inside me that was far beyond the usual teenage angst. I kept it bottled up, though, most of the time. The face I presented to the outside world was one of indifference and I think most people just thought I was odd and disaffected – and perhaps that's what made me an easy target for the school bullies. And once the bullying starts, it becomes a vicious circle: the more I was bullied, the angrier I became; and the angrier I was, the more oddly I behaved; so then I was bullied even more …

On one occasion, I was thrown over a wall by a couple of girls. I was skinny and small for my age, and they just picked me up bodily and tossed me over it. I was bruised and cut, but otherwise not badly hurt, physically at least. Another time my head was pushed down into the bowl of a toilet, which was then flushed repeatedly, until I thought I really was going to drown. And one day some girls held me down while another one cut the hair off on one side of my head. I had to have all my hair cut short after that, and when my father saw it, he was furious. He'd always insisted that my hair should be allowed to grow, and it had been long ever since I was a very little girl. I hated it short too, because as well as being skinny, I'd remained flat-chested long after all the other girls had started to develop, so all it took to make me look like a boy – and, in my mind at least, even uglier than I already felt – was a boy's haircut.

Understandably perhaps, I hated school. I'd drag my feet along the pavement every morning, praying that something – anything – would happen so that I wouldn't ever arrive at the school gates, and feeling increasingly sick and anxious with every step I took. I dreaded waking up in the mornings so much that, eventually, I stopped going to school at all. For six months, I got up at the same time every weekday as I'd always done, got dressed in my school uniform, had my breakfast and left the house at the usual time. But, instead of going to school, I'd walk to the local swimming pool, where I'd sit for hours, watching people swimming.

I Remember, Daddy

My mother never suspected a thing. So she was completely surprised and shocked when the authorities contacted her and said, 'Your daughter hasn't been going to school for weeks.' I think by that time, though, my anger and odd behaviour had already worn her down and, as she'd never been very good at handling crises anyway, she phoned my father and said, 'I can't deal with her. You're going to have to do something.'

That's when my father finally agreed to put his hand in his pocket and pay for something that might be of help to me, and I started attending a private girls' school. I failed my entrance exam, and presumably my father had to pull some strings and call in a few favours to get me in at all. And then things didn't get off to a great start, because I'd missed so much at my last school that I was put in the class below the one I should have been in. It was clear that I had a lot to catch up on, and when everyone else was doing PE, I had to do extra maths and – ironically, in view of all those fables I'd learned – French tuition.

To me, it all seemed like a huge waste of energy and I couldn't really be bothered. I realise now that my lethargy was born of depression. But, at the time, I just accepted the view of most of my teachers – that I was lazy and perhaps a bit stupid.

Another thing that didn't help my situation at the school was the fact that my father never paid the fees on time, if at all. He was always a term or two behind with the payments, which were often made in the end by my mother's parents to avoid my being kicked out. At the time, I probably didn't thank them for intervening to keep me there, although I think I did realise that I might be running out of options if I was asked to leave.

Unfortunately, though, the fact that my father was paying school fees for me – nominally if not always in reality – meant that he began to take more of an active interest in my academic progress, or lack of it. One day, after seeing my end-of-term report, he summoned me to his house. Why he was particularly enraged on that occasion I don't know, because all my reports were pretty bad.

My friend Megan went with me for moral support, and because I hoped my father might not rant and rave so much if someone else was there with me. But, almost as soon as we walked into his house, he flew into a rage and started screaming and swearing at me.

'I'm paying all that money to give you a decent education,' he bellowed, without even the slightest hint of irony or embarrassment, 'and all you can do is fuck about wasting your time and everyone else's. Perhaps you're just stupid. I've always suspected you probably were.'

I Remember, Daddy

He was working himself up into an even worse temper and I was finding it increasingly difficult to look as though I didn't care and wasn't afraid.

'The truth is that you're a lazy little slut,' he shouted, punching my shoulder with his clenched fist and sending me toppling backwards against the kitchen table. 'Get out! Go on, get out of my house!'

Megan was terrified. She gave a little whimper and scurried ahead of me to the front door, where she glanced quickly at me over her shoulder before running down the stone steps on to the pavement. I was just stepping out through the doorway behind her when my father suddenly grabbed hold of me with both hands and flung me down the steps, head first.

Megan gave a squeal of alarm as my face hit the pavement, and when I stood up again she was looking at me, wide-eyed with shock and with her hand over her mouth. The skin on my face was scraped and bleeding and I could taste the metallic taste of blood in my mouth. But I was determined not to give my father the satisfaction of seeing that I was hurt. So I turned away from him and walked down the road beside Megan, limping slightly, with my back straight and my head held high.

In many ways, I hated the new school even more than I'd hated the last one. I'd been used to wearing miniskirts and make-up, and I loathed having to put on my horrible, ugly school uniform every morning. There was one thing that *was* better there than it had been at my previous school though, and that was the fact that I was no longer bullied. Instead, I became the bully. I didn't do anything too terrible – no throwing people over walls or flushing their heads down toilets. It was just that, as almost all the other girls were nicely behaved, respectful and obedient – at least when the teachers were around – my rebellious anger made them instinctively wary of me, and I exploited their wariness.

I set up an ear-piercing business in the toilets, for which I charged £1 a time, and I had plenty of takers. I smoked, I stole from the local shop, and then I began to realise I was becoming someone I didn't recognise. I was doing things that weren't really *me*, although I didn't know why I was doing them and I didn't know how to stop. It felt as though I could never drop my guard, because I was always fighting an invisible enemy.

I still thought everything bad that ever happened to me was my fault. People say that good things happen to good people, so it seemed to make sense that bad things only happen to you if you're a bad person. I know now that that isn't true – good and bad things happen to anyone. But, at the time, whenever anything went wrong for me, I thought I was being punished and that I deserved to be miserable and depressed.

I Remember, Daddy

I used to wish there was someone who could help me. I think if there'd been a ChildLine or something similar in those days, I'd definitely have called them, if only to ask whether they thought I was really mad, as I strongly suspected I was. There was no one to talk to, though, and no one to ask for advice. So I drank and smoked and told myself I didn't care.

The first time I got really drunk was when I was 13. I was at a party at a friend's house and we raided her parents' drinks cupboard. I drank a whole bottle of Pernod, and a couple of my friends had to half-drag, half-carry me home, where they dropped me on the ground outside the front door, rang the bell of the flat and ran away. I was really sick. My mother called the doctor, who said I had alcohol poisoning, and I was in bed for three days.

You'd have thought an experience like that might have made me vow never to touch alcohol again, but it didn't. I started going to pubs after that. How I ever got served I don't know, because I really did look like a young boy. I'd usually go with Jenny, who was pretty and looked older, and who was the one who went up to the bar to buy the drinks. By the time we were 14, we were going to pubs and clubs every Friday and Saturday night, drinking copious amounts of cider and Babycham, and getting drunk.

My mother knew I was drinking and smoking, but she didn't say anything to try to stop me. I think she was just thankful I was coming home at night, and not hanging out on street corners. And she knew I'd do it anyway, whatever she said to me. Perhaps, too, she was grateful for the fact that I was starting to enjoy my life – for the first time that I could remember.

I began to make lots of friends – mostly girls from other schools – and I ended up staying with one of them for a while. Her name was Julia. I shared her bedroom in the flat she lived in with her mother, who often worked away from the city for days at a time, leaving us with the place to ourselves, and who let us do pretty much what we wanted even when she was there. When she wasn't, we'd hold parties and cook bacon and eggs for breakfast and pretend we were adults living an exciting, independent life.

I was still rebellious and strange-looking. Like a lot of young people I think, I felt unattractive, so I tried to make my 'oddness' seem like a positive choice by wearing unconventional clothes and outlandish make-up. There must have been a childlike vulnerability visible beneath my tough exterior, though, because Julia's mother – as well as the mothers of some of my other friends – felt sorry for me and treated me like an adopted daughter.

I Remember, Daddy

There was a group of about 40 of us from different schools who'd meet up every weekend to drink and talk about the boys we were madly in love with that particular week. I was never one of the most popular girls; that honour belonged to two tall, slim, stunningly beautiful girls who were lusted after by all the boys. But I was part of their circle, and I could never quite believe how lucky I was. It felt as though I was part of something at last and, at the weekends at least, I was sometimes almost happy.

Weekdays were a different story, though, and I still did stupid things that were almost designed to get me into trouble and to test to the limits the tolerance of the school, as well as of my mother.

After school sometimes, I'd go with my friend Lucinda to a local record shop, where we'd steal little metal badges that were popular at the time and that everyone used to buy to pin on their school bags. Eventually, we'd taken so many we had to hide them, and we put them in Lucinda's desk at school, which is where they were when, one day, without thinking, Lucinda opened the lid of her desk just as the teacher came to stand beside her.

'Well, well, what have we here?' the teacher asked, picking up a handful of the badges and letting them slip through her fingers. 'Where did these come from?'

'From the shop, Miss.' Lucinda looked down at her desk.

'I realise that, Lucinda.' The teacher's tone was sarcastic. 'I didn't imagine for one moment that you'd done anything as industrious as making them yourself, or that you'd found them hanging on a tree somewhere. To whom do they belong?'

Lucinda glanced sideways towards me and pulled an apologetic face before answering, 'They're mine, Miss. And Katie's.'

'I see.' The teacher was one of several who didn't like me, and she gave a small, satisfied smile. 'So, let me repeat my original question. Where did these come from? Did you and Katie purchase them yourselves, with your own hard-earned money?'

'No, Miss. We ...' Lucinda's face was red with embarrassment and shame. 'We nicked them, Miss.'

A brief ripple of laughter ran around the classroom, punctuated by gasps from a couple of the girls who were more easily shocked. I doubt, though, whether anyone was really surprised to discover that *I* was a shoplifter, as I'm sure that, in their minds, it was just one short step from non-conformity to theft.

'Silence!' the teacher roared, turning to glare ferociously around the room. 'This is no laughing matter. Stealing is a very serious, *criminal*, offence.' She scowled at me as she emphasised the word, and then added, 'You will stay behind at the end of the lesson – both of you.'

After school, Lucinda and I went to the record shop with our teacher to return the stolen badges and apologise. Luckily, the manager of the shop decided not to prosecute us, although he did ban us from the premises – 'for ever' – and I was expelled from school.

In fact, it wasn't the first time I'd been expelled – nor was it to be the last – and, as on all the previous occasions, I was allowed back after my father sent the school a substantial cheque. I think there were quite a few teachers who must have wished he had less money, because most of them hated me, probably with good reason. It was a school with traditional values and rules and, in addition to not doing very well academically, I used to turn up in the mornings wearing make-up, with my hair dyed lurid colours and the top of my skirt rolled up around my waist, transforming it from sedate knee-length uniform into a strip of material that only just covered my bottom. I saw my behaviour as expressing my quirky individuality and my refusal blindly to conform. But I know that, to most of my teachers, I was just a tiresome pain in the neck.

I think the headmistress liked me, though. Whenever she saw me on the street wearing make-up that was far too obvious to be ignored or a non-regulation scarf or jacket, she'd sigh and say, 'Katie. My office.

Tomorrow.' Then she'd wait patiently as I took off the offending object and put it into her outstretched hand. But the corners of her mouth would always twitch, as though she was suppressing a smile, and her eyes would be amused and kind rather than angrily impatient, as the other teachers always were. And I think that, even when my father was late paying my school fees, the headmistress always fought my corner.

The teacher I hated more than anyone was my geography teacher, primarily because she made it very clear in every way possible that she hated me. She was always telling me, 'You'll never do well in life.' But, however hard I worked to try to prove to her that I wasn't lazy and useless, she refused to acknowledge my efforts.

Everything came to a head one day when we had a test. I'd revised for it until I was answering questions in my sleep, and a few days later, when the teacher handed out our marked papers in class, mine was on the top of the pile.

I couldn't believe that I'd got the best mark. I stared at the number that was written in red ink at the top of the page: 94%! I could feel my cheeks burning red with pride and a sense of satisfaction at the thought that all my hard work had been worthwhile. Perhaps I wasn't stupid after all; maybe if I did work hard, I could do as well as the other girls, or even better.

I Remember, Daddy

The geography teacher used to give little presents to girls who got good scores in tests. On that day, however, she just handed my paper to me without a word and then turned to praise the girl who'd come second. I looked down quickly at my desk to hide the tears of disappointed embarrassment that had sprung into my eyes, and when I looked up again, one of my friends had raised her hand.

The teacher looked in her direction and arched her eyebrows quizzically.

'Did Katie Matthews get the top mark, Miss?' my friend asked.

'Yes. She did.' The teacher almost snapped her reply. Then, turning to hand a paper to another girl, she added over her shoulder to my friend, 'It's a shame your own mark wasn't as good.'

'But ... If Katie got the best mark, why didn't you say anything to her, Miss?' my friend persisted. 'You always say something to the girl who comes first. So why not ...'

The teacher interrupted her, her face flushed with irritation. 'That's enough, thank you. I don't need ...'

It was my turn to interrupt. I scraped my chair noisily across the floor, pushing it away from my desk as I stood up and shouted, 'I've had enough of you. You can just fuck off.'

For a split-second the teacher was too shocked to respond. Then she threw the pile of remaining papers down on the desk in front of her, raised one arm, pointed with her index finger towards the door and bellowed, 'Out! Get out of my classroom Katherine Matthews.'

'Don't worry, I'm going,' I shouted back at her, grabbing the bag that was hanging over the back of my chair and sweeping everything off my desk into it with one angry movement of my arm. 'I'm going to the headmistress, and I'm going to tell her about you. And I'm not coming back to your stupid geography classes ever again. You can stuff them.'

I stormed out of the classroom and marched down the corridor to the headmistress's study, where I knocked on the door.

The headmistress regarded me steadily as I told her what had happened. Then she shook her head and said with a sigh, 'What am I going to do with you, Katie? You know what this means, don't you.'

'I suppose I'm going to get expelled again,' I answered, sighing deeply myself at the thought of all the shouting and arguing I would have to endure when my father and mother found out what had happened.

To my surprise, however, the headmistress almost smiled as she said, 'No. I'm not going to expel you

– again – although I know that's what you'd like me to do. You won't, of course, be able to return to any geography lessons. So, instead, you can do extra maths and French.'

Starting with my father when I was a very small child, everyone always seemed to be telling me that I'd never get anywhere in my life. My headmistress didn't seem to agree with them, but some of my teachers voiced the opinion that it was hardly worth my taking my 'O' levels. And one day I suddenly got sick of all their negative opinions of me and thought, 'Just you watch me,' and I settled down to catch up on all the work I'd missed, ending up taking five exams and passing all of them – four with A grades.

Despite my unexpected academic success, however, I still hated school. I hated having to follow rules that seemed pointless and without any real purpose other than to make us do whatever we were told. I'd spent my whole life doing what I was told, and now there was something inside me that was rebelling and questioning everything, something that prevented me ever being able to relax and just go with the flow. It was a tension, a type of latent aggression, that seemed to make me constantly dissatisfied, and I didn't understand why. What I did know, though, was that I couldn't bear to stay on at school a moment longer after I'd taken my exams. So, just before my 16th birthday, I persuaded my mother to persuade the school to let me leave, and I started working full-time at the shop where I'd had a Saturday job for the last couple of years.

The following year, when I was 17, my brother moved in to live with my mother and me for a while. We'd spent so little time together over the years that I felt as though I barely knew my brother, and it was clear that he felt the same disconnect with me. We fought almost constantly, until one day my mother told me, 'I can't cope with your behaviour any more. You're going to have to go and stay with your father.'

Although he'd stopped sexually abusing me some five years earlier, I was still afraid of my father. But by that time I didn't care what happened to me or where I was sent to live, so I moved into his house and stayed there for a few months.

Sally had just left him. As well as being feisty, she was a realist, and whereas I just pretended to be tough, she really was as hard as nails. She wasn't a woman who would ever have allowed herself to be bullied and coerced by anyone and, despite myself, I always rather liked her, particularly when I discovered that she'd taken literally everything with her when she'd gone, including every single light bulb in the house.

In contrast to my mother, who used to cower and whimper whenever my father attacked her, Sally would attack him right back again, hitting him over the head with a pan or whatever came to hand whenever he had a go at her. I admired her for that, and I often wondered why my father – who would, quite literally, turn puce with rage if any of us every argued with him – put up with it. I suppose the answer was that he was a bully and, as with all bullies, all it needed was for someone to stand up to him.

Sally and my father came from the same sort of background and they understood each other. When he married my mother, my father had a game plan – to be rich and successful and to 'move up in the world' – and I think he hated the fact that my mother belonged naturally to the world he aspired to be part of. So, to correct the balance and assert a superiority he maybe didn't entirely feel, he intimidated and abused her. And she didn't fight back, because she was already timid and unsure of herself when they met, and because, for whatever reason, she loved him.

My father had controlled and brainwashed me into obeying him from a very early age and, like my mother, I accepted the reflection of myself that I saw in his eyes – in my case, because I knew no differently. But Sally had a mind of her own; she could be as harsh and determined as my father was, and he knew that she wouldn't be afraid to use any information she had against him – and against his friends – if he pushed her too far. So, when their marriage broke up, instead of charging her rent to live in a dismal flat in one of the worst parts of town, as he'd done to my mother, he bought her a house and a small business, and they remained friends.

However, my father wasn't a man to be without a woman for long, and after Sally left he soon turned his attentions to Gillian, who was not much older than I was. For a long time, he persisted in pretending she was 'just helping me with some work I'm doing', which was a lie that was both embarrassing and totally unnecessary, because the true nature of their relationship was clear to everyone.

One night, my father took Gillian and me out for dinner, and we were having a drink in a pub afterwards when a man came in and greeted him effusively. My father introduced him to Gillian as Bradley, a friend of his who owned a popular nightclub in town. I'd heard my father talk about him before, and I knew that he'd been arrested for something – I couldn't remember what – but that, because he had friends in influential circles, he'd gone to court but not to prison.

'And who's this?' the man asked, sitting down next to me and leaning a bit too close towards me.

'This is my daughter, er … Katie,' my father told him, pretending – or perhaps not – that he'd had to think for a moment to remember my name.

I Remember, Daddy

'She's very pretty.' Bradley smiled a lewd smile that showed a row of uneven, yellow teeth. He looked like something out of a low-budget porn film – fat and ugly, with long, curly, dirty-blond hair and a very unattractive moustache.

'You can have her for a tenner,' my father told him, leaning forward in his chair to take a swig from his glass of whisky and smirking at me.

'Pardon?' I asked my father.

I could feel the heat of humiliation burning my cheeks. But he ignored me and spoke again to his friend. 'I said you can have her for a tenner, Bradley. If you want her, take her.'

I'd thought at first that he was making a tasteless joke, but there was no hint of humour in his voice, and I realised with a sick feeling that he was completely serious. He was actually offering his own 17-year-old daughter to a sleazy, criminal nightclub owner.

I was furious. When I was young, my father used to tell me that the only 'useful' thing women were capable of doing was spreading their legs, and it was clearly an opinion he still held.

'You're unbelievable,' I told him, pushing back my chair and standing up.

I looked down at him coldly for a moment and then walked away from him towards the door. Gillian followed me out of the pub, and a few seconds later my father came out too, laughing and joking with someone who'd held the door open for him.

As soon as the car was moving, Gillian asked my father, 'How could you do that? That was horrible. It was so embarrassing for Katie.' Then she burst into tears.

My father didn't answer her, but I could sense his anger as we drove back to his house in silence.

I didn't want to give him the satisfaction of knowing how upset I was, so I went straight to the bathroom, and as I came out again I could hear him shouting at Gillian, 'Don't *ever* question anything I do. And don't *ever* cry in front of my daughter again!'

I felt sorry for her. What my father had said in the pub had infuriated and hurt me, but it hadn't shocked me. It was just the way he was, and there was nothing anyone was ever going to be able to do to change him. Clearly, though, it *had* shocked Gillian, and I knew she'd just learned her first lesson about what would happen if she questioned or argued with my father.

I knew I couldn't live at his house any longer after that. I left a few days later and moved in to the first of a series of rooms in other people's flats that I rented over the next few months.

Eleven

A few months later, when I was 18, I spent the summer working in a seaside town with my friend Jenny. We rented a couple of rooms in a house that was owned and lived in by a man and his son, although they were hardly ever there and we often had the place to ourselves for days at a time. It all seemed like an adventure. The town was popular with holiday-makers, so there were plenty of jobs to be had during the summer, and we both started work almost immediately after we arrived – Jenny in a café/restaurant and me in a pub. Then we settled down to earn some money and enjoy the sun, sea and sense of freedom we both felt at being footloose, fancy-free and far away from home.

There were lots of other young people working the summer season, and we soon made friends. Because there was no one there who knew me – apart from Jenny, who I could trust not to talk about me to anyone – I felt as though, for the first time in my life, *I* could decide who I was and what I wanted to tell people about myself. Although I could never completely lose my sense of underlying guilt and anxiety, it was liberating to get away from my real life for a while and from all the baggage and complications that went with it.

One of the people I became friends with was a girl called Issie. She was seven months' pregnant when I met her, and her boyfriend, Dan, was the manager of the pub where I was working. Issie was a really lovely girl, sweet-natured and pretty and clearly besotted by Dan, who seemed to be just as in love with her, too. So, on the couple of occasions when Dan tried to kiss me, I brushed it off, told him not to be so daft and assumed he was just messing around.

Then, one night, when I finished work late, after everyone else had already left the pub, Dan offered to walk me home. He was locking up as I was leaving and so we set off together, past the few drunks who were still out on the streets and along the road that led to the house where I was staying. We talked about some of the people who'd been in the pub that night, and about the preparations he and Issie were making for the birth of their baby, and when we got to the house, he asked if he could come in to phone for a taxi to take him the rest of the way home.

As I turned my key in the front door, the house was in darkness. The owner and his son were away, and clearly Jenny was having a late night out too. So I turned on the hall light, showed Dan where the phone was and then went upstairs to the bathroom.

When I came out, Dan was standing outside the bathroom door and I almost jumped out of my skin.

'God, you gave me a fright, lurking there in the darkness,' I told him. 'Did you get a taxi okay? Come on, I'll make some coffee while we're waiting.'

I waited for him to turn and walk back down the stairs ahead of me. But he just stood there and asked, 'Which is your room?'

'It's down there,' I said, pointing vaguely down the landing. 'It's a nice house, isn't it? We were lucky to find it. Come on. I'll put the kettle on.'

Suddenly, Dan lunged at me, grabbed me by the shoulders and tried to kiss me.

'Jesus, Dan,' I said, twisting my head from side to side as I tried to shake him off. 'Cut it out! What the hell are you doing?'

'Come on, Katie. You know you want it.' There was a nasty edge to his voice that I'd never heard before.

'Of course I don't bloody *want it*.' I began to feel sick. 'Issie's my friend, and she's *your* girlfriend and about to become the mother of your child. Forget it, Dan. Let's just make some coffee.'

I tried to push him away, but he grasped my arms, digging his fingers painfully into my skin as he half-carried, half-dragged me along the landing and kicked open my bedroom door. I struggled wildly, trying to elbow him in the stomach, but it was as though he couldn't even feel it.

'For Christ's sake!' I shouted at him. But he just threw me on to the bed, and when I saw the cruel, sneering expression on his face and the blank emptiness in his eyes, I began to feel really afraid.

As he flung himself down on top of me, I tried to twist my body underneath his so that I could raise my knee and kick him. But I couldn't move.

'Stop it. Please. I don't want this.' For a moment I could hear my mother's voice pleading with my father. A single sob rose up from somewhere deep inside me, and it was as though I could feel the same sense of hopelessness and humiliation she must have felt so many times while they were married.

Dan pinned me to the bed with his knees, pulled up my skirt and ripped off my underwear. And then he raped me, while I lay underneath him, crying like a child. For a split-second I thought I saw my father's face looking down at me and heard his voice saying, 'This is your fault: bad things only happen to bad people.'

I Remember, Daddy

When Dan had finished, he stood up, pulled on his underpants and jeans and walked out of the room without a word. I turned towards the wall and pulled the sheet up over me, pressing my face into the pillow, too numb and exhausted even to cry any more.

Although I didn't hear the front door shut, I assumed that Dan had left the house, until, a few seconds later, I heard a sound and turned my head to see him standing in the doorway of my bedroom. He was holding a wooden-handled floor brush and he smiled a cold, scornful smile as he snatched the sheet that was covering me and threw it on to the floor. Then he held me down on the bed as he forced the handle of the brush inside me. It felt as though fire was shooting up through my body, and I screamed as I tried to twist away from him.

I must have blacked out, because the next thing I remember is hearing the front door slam and opening my eyes to find myself alone in my bedroom. I dropped one arm over the side of the bed, dragged the sheet across my shivering body and began to sob.

I don't know how long I'd been lying there, unaware of everything except for the intense pain that seemed to be burning inside me, when I heard a noise downstairs. I held my breath to listen. There was definitely someone in the house; Dan hadn't gone after all. I started to whimper like a cowed, frightened dog and had to bite my lip to stop myself crying out as panic surged through my body. I pulled the sheet over my head, the way I used to do when I was a child, and began to pray, 'Please, God, don't let him see me.'

But it was Jenny, not Dan, who opened my bedroom door and whispered, 'Katie, are you awake?'

I lowered the sheet and turned slowly to look at her, and she gasped.

'God, Katie, what's up?' she asked, sitting down on the edge of my bed and gently touching my tear-stained face. 'Are you ill?'

'I … I've got a terrible pain,' I told her. 'In my stomach.'

'You look awful,' she said. 'How long have you been like this? I'm going to call an ambulance.'

'No!' I tried to sit up, but it felt as though someone had removed every single bone in my body, and I flopped back again on to the pillow. 'No, I don't need an ambulance. I just want …' I breathed in sharply as a great wave of pain washed over me.

'I'm sorry.' Jenny stood up. 'I really do think you need to go to hospital. You might have appendicitis.'

Before I could protest again, she'd left the room and I could hear her talking on the telephone in the hallway.

With Jenny's help, I managed to walk to the bath-room, where I washed away the blood from between my legs. Then we sat together in the living room, waiting for the ambulance to arrive.

I said nothing to anyone about what had happened, and for the next few days I was kept in hospital while they did tests, and then scratched their heads in bafflement at what could possibly be causing such acute and clearly agonising pain. Having ruled out appendicitis, it was decided that I must have a urinary tract infection. So they gave me antibiotics as well as painkillers. And still I said nothing, because I was filled with a sense of shame and guilt that I didn't understand, but that was so overwhelming it made me wish I could just curl up and die.

The day after I'd been admitted to the hospital, one of Dan's friends came to see me. I'd seen him in the pub a couple of times, but I didn't know him very well, and as he was an unlikely and unexpected visitor, I didn't immediately recognise him when I saw him walking down the ward. So I was surprised when he stopped by my bed and said, 'How ya doing?'

'Are you here to see me?' I asked him.

He nodded.

'Why? Why have you come?' But, before he had time to answer, I added, 'It doesn't matter. I don't want to talk to you anyway. Please, just leave me alone.'

'It's okay,' he told me. 'I've just come to see how you're doing – and to bring you this.' He held out towards me what looked like a bit of rolled-up paper and winked.

'Take it,' he said, shaking it briefly under my nose and then trying to thrust it into my hand. 'It'll calm you down.'

Suddenly I realised it was a joint.

'I'm in a hospital for God's sake!' I hissed, turning my head away from his outstretched hand and glancing nervously around the ward, anxious in case anyone else could see what he was holding. 'I don't want it. I don't smoke that stuff anyway.'

'Yeah, but this is a special occasion,' he grinned. 'People use it as medicine when they're not well. It'll do you good.'

I clenched my fists and looked away from him, and eventually he shrugged and slipped the joint into the pocket of his jacket.

'Have you told anyone about what happened?' he asked, walking over to the window beside my bed and leaning forward slightly so that he could look down into the street below.

I didn't answer.

'I'm guessing you haven't,' he continued after a moment. 'And I just wanted to tell you that you're doing the right thing. Dan's been in trouble before, see. So he could go to prison if you start blabbing. And then poor old Issie's baby wouldn't have a father. I know Issie's your friend, and you wouldn't want to do that to her. Would you? Besides, what happened was your fault really. All those short skirts you girls wear.' He turned away from the window and leered. 'You're just asking for it.'

His tone was chattily matter-of-fact. Perhaps he was too stoned to be aggressive, or perhaps he was so sure I'd agree with his point of view and accept responsibility for what his friend had done to me that there was no need for him even to raise his voice. He didn't have to worry, though. I already felt guilty and tainted by what Dan had done. I just wanted to block it out of my mind and pretend it had never happened. And I certainly didn't want to talk to anyone about it, not even my best friend Jenny.

A few days later, when I was discharged from the hospital, I went back to the house, packed up my things and got a train home. I'd already spoken on the phone to my mother, so she knew I'd been in hospital, although she didn't know why. She must have been concerned about how low and depressed I sounded, though, because apparently as soon as I'd rung off she phoned my father. It was one of the periods when they were talking to each other, and she told him how worried she was about me and asked if there was any chance that he could pay for me to have a holiday.

'Perfect timing!' my father told her cheerfully. 'I've rented a place for the week, for the Test match. She can come with me.'

A few days later, I travelled with Gillian – who, for some reason, my father was still pretending was just his 'researcher' – to stay at the large house he'd rented in the countryside near the city where the Test match was going to take place. The plan was that Gillian and I would be there on our own for a couple of days and then he'd drive down at the weekend.

I quite liked Gillian, and we had a pleasant, fairly relaxed couple of days together. Then, on the day my father was due to arrive, it was an hour or two before we were expecting him and I was smoking in the living room when I heard a car pull up on the gravel drive. Gillian immediately flew into a panic.

'Oh my God! What are we going to do?' she screeched, wafting her hand backwards and forwards in front of my cigarette. 'That's your dad! He hates people smoking. Quick, put the cigarette out. Oh my God!'

Clearly, my father's relationship with Gillian was more similar to the one he'd had with my mother than with Sally.

Although I'd vowed to myself that I would no longer allow my father to unnerve and undermine me, I couldn't help catching Gillian's sense of hysteria. I stubbed out the cigarette in the ashtray on the coffee table and then pushed it under the sofa, while Gillian continued to wave her arms around like someone sending crazy semaphore messages.

As it turned out, though, she was right to be afraid, because as soon as my father walked into the house, he stopped, tilted his head back slightly, sniffed a couple of times and said, 'Who's been smoking?'

Gillian and I were almost quaking with fear, but I managed to find my tongue first.

'Oh, it was the handyman,' I told my father, trying to sound casual but disapproving. 'He had one in his hand when he came in to fix something or other.'

'Well, tell him not to smoke in the house again,' my father snapped, and I felt Gillian slowly releasing the breath she'd been holding.

The house was beautiful, and massive, and I wondered why my father had rented somewhere with so many rooms for just the three of us. Then, later that same day, the doorbell rang, heralding the arrival of the first of all the friends he'd invited to stay – several of them men I'd known as a child.

I felt stupid and embarrassed for having believed that my father had been concerned for my well-being and that he'd wanted to give me a holiday. Because it soon became clear that I wasn't there for a holiday at all; I was there to help Gillian in her role as chief cook and bottle-washer. Almost every day for the rest of the week, she and I bought food, prepared vegetables and cooked for all my father's guests. And when we weren't stuck in the kitchen, cooking and washing up, he expected us always to be at his beck and call.

My common sense told me to shrug it off and just *do* it, because I shouldn't have expected anything better from my father and, actually, it didn't matter anyway. But I couldn't help feeling hurt and disappointed because, despite years of experience that should have told me otherwise, I'd allowed myself to think that he might finally have decided he liked me enough to want to spend some time with me.

One of the men who came to stay at the house for a few days was a man called Bernard, a friend of my father who I couldn't stand. He was an alcoholic – like most of my father's friends – and it was alcohol that killed him not long afterwards. In fact, the only 'normal' people staying there were a very nice elderly couple, who seemed a bit overwhelmed by it all and who went to bed early every night. Everyone else was loud, self-absorbed, chauvinistic and just vile.

One evening, when I was having a bath, three of my father's friends broke down the door and came crashing into the bathroom, drunk and giggling like schoolboys. I screamed and tried to cover myself with my arms, shouting at them to get out. And eventually, still laughing and cracking lewd jokes, they left, stumbling and falling over each other as they staggered out through the doorway. I was 18 years old and the men were in their forties and fifties, at least; but, afterwards, it was me my father was furious with.

'These are *my* guests,' he bellowed at me. 'How dare you complain about them? You will do *whatever* they want you to do. Do you understand?'

Basically, what my father was telling me was that if any of his friends wanted to sleep with me, it was not only okay with him, but he'd actually be angry if I refused. It was several years before I was to remember what he'd allowed – and encouraged – his friends to do to me as a child, so I was totally shocked by what he was saying. But I was too frightened of him to argue. Instead, I made a silent promise to myself that I would never, ever, let any of his disgusting drunken friends lay their hands on me, however angry that might make him.

It soon became clear that there was one particular man my father was trying to pair me off with. His name was Tony and he was in his forties, rich and ugly. It was obvious he liked me, and one evening at dinner my father told him, conversationally, 'You know, you can have my daughter if you want her. It's fine with me.' He was completely serious, and Tony was delighted as he turned to leer at me drunkenly and said, 'Ooh, yes please!'

I stared back at him coldly as I muttered, 'I don't think so,' and the men around the dinner table laughed. Later, though, my father followed me out into the kitchen, leaned towards me until his face was just a couple of inches away from mine and hissed, 'You'll bloody well do whatever it takes to please Tony.'

It was the way he'd always treated me: I didn't matter, and what I wanted didn't matter, because the only thing that was important was what my father wanted. As he stood there, breathing alcohol fumes into my face, I felt my heart sink, because I knew that I was still too afraid of him to fight back. Fortunately, though, I was saved from being prostituted out to my father's friend by another man I met while I was staying in the house – a German called Karl.

Unlike my father's sleazy friend Tony, Karl was lovely. And because he was rich and well connected, my father allowed him to come to the house to 'court' me, as he called it, and to take me out for walks. Karl really was a nice man, and as we talked and laughed together, I felt grateful to have someone to keep me company who wasn't one of my father's old drunken friends.

During that week, we'd sometimes all go out to restaurants, and at the end of the meal my father would pick up the bill. He never had bank accounts – or, at least, the money he used for day-to-day expenses, which had been paid to him in cash, never went into a bank account. Gillian used to carry around for him in her handbag a large padded envelope full of £50 notes, and sometimes it would be tossed casually on to a table and he'd wave his hand towards it and tell me, 'Help yourself. Take what you want. Go and buy some champagne.' But he only ever did it to show off when someone else was there, because in reality he never gave me anything. In restaurants, though, he'd put his hand into the envelope and start pulling out notes to pay the bill, and on at least a couple of occasions during that week he happily paid £600 or more for everyone's meal – which was a lot of money in the early 1980s. And then all his friends laughed and raised their glasses to drink his very good health.

The only effect his ostentatious open-handedness had on me, however, was to make me feel irritated and resentful, because when I was a child and my mother couldn't afford to buy me clothes, he wouldn't even give her enough money to pay for a pair of shoes for me. And, a couple of years after that 'holiday', when I was destitute and asked him for £20, he refused to help me and shouted at me, 'I have no money.' To him, money was the means of getting what *he* wanted, as well as a reason for his friends – and total strangers – to admire him. So what was the point of giving it to his daughter when there was no one there to witness his generosity?

My father didn't watch much of the cricket during that week – and nor did most of the people who stayed with us. It was really just an excuse for him to be seen to be the host of lavish entertainment.

Everyone drank champagne, so I drank it too and my father seemed happy for me to do so. Then, one evening we went to a pub and he told me to sit outside.

'But, Dad,' I told him, 'I'm 18. It's okay. I can go inside a pub.'

'No,' he said, in the sort of firm, clear voice you might use to instruct a potentially naughty child. He pointed towards a table and a solitary seat in the garden. 'You will sit there until we come out.'

Like most of the things he did, it was designed to control and humiliate me, and I knew there was no point arguing. So I sat alone in the pub garden, waiting and wondering why I'd ever thought anything would have changed.

Over the next few months, as my father acknowledged his true relationship with Gillian, he gradually re-modelled her in the image of my mother – with short, sculpted, chestnut-brown hair (dyed, in Gillian's case), smart, well-cut clothes and understated but expensive jewellery. Gillian was young and quite attractive, and I simply couldn't see what she saw in my father. So, one day, I asked her. She looked terrified and glanced anxiously behind her as though she was afraid we might be overheard. Then she just shrugged and changed the subject.

I suppose, though, that he could be charming and good company when he wanted to be, and he had money, which meant she was leading a life she couldn't otherwise have afforded – living in a lovely home, eating meals at good restaurants, holidaying in expensive hotels and rubbing shoulders with some of the city's most influential men. Perhaps, in exchange for all that, she was prepared to put up with my father's bullying and depravity – although, to me, it seemed to be far too high a price to pay, whatever the perceived rewards. But maybe she'd already heard the door of the trap snap shut behind her and felt unable to get out. Or maybe she simply loved him and, like my mother had done for so many years, felt that one day, if she tried hard enough, she might actually please him.

I didn't see my father very often after that week I spent with him and Gillian and all his drunken friends. In fact, the next time I saw him was a few months later, when I was working in a bar in town and he came in one evening and asked if a friend of his was already there. He spoke to me as though I was a total stranger, and I realised he hadn't recognised me – or perhaps he was just pretending not to have done so, for some stupid, theatrically childish reason of his own.

'Dad, it's me!' I said, trying not to sound irritated. 'Your daughter.'

He looked at me, raised his eyebrows and shrugged as he said, 'Oh, yes … *Well*, is he here?'

I was hurt, even though part of me realised he'd said it for dramatic effect and because he enjoyed being spiteful. I always felt as though I had to try to prove myself to him, to show him I wasn't the useless failure and waste of space who couldn't do anything right that he'd always told me I was when I was a child. I always hoped that one day he'd notice me and like me. It was never going to happen; but it was that same need to prove myself that eventually became the driving force behind my success at work.

Working in the bar was just a stopgap, to earn some extra money. I also had a job as a junior assistant in a shop, and within a couple of years I'd become its manager. With an annual salary of £7,000 – which was good money at the time – I was able to buy my first flat when I was 21.

But, however well I did, I still felt like an imposter – as though I was acting the part of someone who had a good job and their own home, while in reality I was waiting for the inevitable moment when something would happen to make everything come crashing down around my ears.

I Remember, Daddy

Very occasionally after I bought the flat, my father would make contact with me, and one day he came to see me and noticed a bill that was open on my kitchen table.

'What's this?' he asked, picking it up and glaring at it.

'It's a bill from my solicitor – to do with buying the flat,' I told him.

'Why haven't you bloody paid it?' he shouted, flapping it in front of my face angrily. 'I'm not just anybody, you know. I've got a reputation in this town, and I can't have my daughter owing money to solicitors.'

'I don't *owe money to solicitors*,' I snapped, reaching out to try to take the bill out of his hand. 'I owe *one* solicitor £400, which I'm going to pay as soon as I can. I just don't have it right at this particular moment.'

Still holding the bill, he stomped into the living room and picked up the telephone, and a few seconds later I heard him say, 'Oh, yes, good morning. This is Harold Matthews. My daughter Katherine is a client of yours. Yes, that's right. Well, I've just discovered she has an outstanding bill with you and I wanted to assure you that it *will* be paid. I'll be paying it myself, within the next few days.'

And he did pay that bill. He hadn't been able to give me £20 when I'd asked him to help me out; he hadn't given my mother money to house, feed and clothe me when I was a child; but he managed to pay my £400 solicitor's bill. And he did it because he knew the solicitor – or, at least, knew *of* him – and, more importantly, because he thought that the solicitor would know about him, and he was anxious not to sully his own carefully cultivated reputation as an affluent local businessman and pillar of society.

My father knew a lot of people, including almost everyone of any consequence in the city. To his friends and colleagues, he was 'good old Harry', fun, witty and good company, and he could certainly captivate people with his eccentric charm and entertaining stories. But what they never saw were his outbursts of rage and his apparent need to lash out and hurt the people who should have been closest to him, and who he should have done almost anything to protect.

Lots of my father's clients – and friends – were crooks and criminals, whose backhanders and dubious under-the-table payments filled and refilled his padded envelope many times over. To my father, almost everything in life was just a game. All that really mattered to him was feeling that he *was* someone – someone important and significant and cleverer than everyone else. And I suppose, in some respects, that's what he was, and that's why he got away with so much for so long, and why still, to this day, he hasn't had to answer for the many dishonest and terrible things he's done.

Unlike my father, though, I was determined to make my way in life honestly and without cheating, so that I could feel proud of anything I managed to achieve. Unfortunately, however, although I was doing well at work, I'd been too emotionally damaged by what my father had done to me to be able to have the same success in my love life.

I was with one boyfriend – my first love – for almost three years. But he cheated on me repeatedly, telling me that I was frigid and that because I wasn't always willing, he had to satisfy his sexual needs with some-one else. And it was true that, for reasons I didn't understand at the time, I didn't really want to have sex. When that relationship broke up, I started going out with Dale. We got engaged almost immediately and were together for six months; and then I was with Mickey for a year.

I was looking for something, although I didn't know what it was, and every time I thought I'd found it, I'd fool myself into believing I was happy. Then, after a while, it would all go wrong again and I'd be heartbroken. I desperately wanted to be loved, but if someone did seem to love me, it just proved that they didn't really know me, because I knew I was unlovable.

I seemed to be constantly on edge, always waiting, and never able to relax and accept things as they were. I never knew why I felt like that, or what it was I was waiting *for*. Perhaps it was just the inevitable effect of having spent almost every minute of my childhood anxiously anticipating the next frightening thing that was going to happen.

Looking back on it now, it was a miracle I was able to find anyone who was prepared to go out with me at all! But when I met Tom, who was patient and good to me, and who loved me and was my best friend, I knew I'd found the person I wanted to be with for ever. And then Sam was born and I began to remember the terrible things my father had done to me when I was a child, and my life fell apart.

TWelve

I 'd been very ill after Sam was born. Nothing could erase the horror of the things I'd been remembering; but knowing that the psychiatrist believed them did help me in my battle to sort out what was real and what wasn't in the peculiar Alice-in-Wonderland world I seemed to have woken up in

Even when I left the hospital, after being there for six months, no one was under any illusion that I was really well again. I knew that recovering was going to be a long, slow process, although I had no idea just how long it was actually going to take.

However, I was better than I had been, although I wasn't fit to go back to work. I was taking medication and needed a lot of support, from social services as well as from Tom, his parents, my mother and good friends like Jenny. Despite all the help I was getting, though, I was still balancing on a knife's edge between just about coping and not coping at all.

Then, not long after Christmas, when I'd been at home for about three months, Sam was rushed into hospital with a collapsed lung and pneumonia. As I sat in the ambulance beside him, I felt as if I was in a dream, watching the events that were unfolding around me but unable to *do* anything or influence what was happening in any way.

The siren of the ambulance as it sped through the streets towards the hospital sounded muffled, as though it was coming from somewhere far in the distance, and I felt completely numb. I couldn't bear to look at Sam's waxy grey face and see his blue lips or watch his tiny fragile chest going up and down, up and down, so fast that he seemed to be panting, although he was barely taking in any air at all. The paramedic moved around him, turning dials and looking at monitors with a sombre expression on his face, while a voice in my head kept whispering, 'Sam might die,' and I had to grip the edge of my seat to stop myself screaming out loud.

Sam spent his first birthday in an oxygen tent, and I sat beside him throughout that day – and throughout all the other days he was in the hospital – watching helplessly as he fought for his life. I couldn't stay with him at night, though, because I wouldn't have been able to keep up the appearance of being normal during the night. I knew that the nurses didn't approve when I went home; they thought I was leaving Sam alone at the hospital so that I could sleep in the comfort of my own bed. But it wasn't that I didn't *want* to be there with him, or that I didn't care enough. It was just that I was afraid of the night-time and I knew I simply couldn't do it. Even during the day, I constantly had to fight the urge to bawl like a baby.

It was clear that there was a very strong chance Sam was going to die, and I thought his death would be *my* fault. I'd always lived with a sense of guilt, for reasons I hadn't understood until the memories of my childhood had started to return. But, instead of making it better, the things I was remembering had made it worse, and I was convinced that Sam's death would be my punishment: bad things happen to bad people and, clearly, Sam himself wasn't bad.

By some miracle, however, Sam survived, and as soon as I knew he was going to live, I let go and started to slip over the edge of reason again into a total breakdown.

Although I wasn't aware of most of what I was doing at the time, people told me afterwards that I'd often appear to regress to childhood. One minute I'd be talking normally and seem fine, and then something would trigger a half-formed memory – even a smell or a word or phrase could do it – and I'd curl up in a ball on the floor in the corner of the room, or sit on the sofa with my knees clutched tightly against my chest, rocking backwards and forwards and talking baby-talk in an eerily childish voice.

All I was aware of was that I was frightened. I knew I had to try to protect myself, but I didn't know what from. So, if anyone came near me at all, I'd lash out and shout, 'Keep away from me! Don't touch me!'

Tom was frightened too – both *for* me and *of* me, I think. He wasn't afraid that I'd hurt anyone, except perhaps myself; but I was unpredictable and my episodes of regressing to childhood were unnerving for anyone who witnessed them. It must have been awful for him. He'd had so much stress during the past few months that my being ill again must have seemed like the last straw. He'd been worried about me when I was in the psychiatric hospital, and about Sam when he was ill, and about how we were going to manage to live on just his income and pay the mortgage while I wasn't able to work. Now he had to worry about me again and about what I might do to myself. And then, one day, I tried to stab him with a knife.

It was late morning and Tom and I were in the kitchen. I was cutting bread and Tom was standing at right-angles to me, just a few feet away, leaning against the sink and glancing occasionally out of the window as he talked. Suddenly, a half-remembered image flashed across my mind. It was of my father in the kitchen of the house where we lived when I was a small child, leaning against the sink and drinking from a crystal glass of whisky. Instantly I was a child again, and as I turned my head to look towards Tom, I saw instead my father's coldly sneering face.

My whole body began to shake violently. I gripped the edge of the work surface and tried to breathe and Tom took a step towards me.

'Are you all right, Katie?' he asked.

He sounded concerned, but the voice in my head was mocking. I raised the knife and lunged at him.

'Jesus, Katie. What the hell are you doing?' Tom twisted his body sideways and the blade narrowly missed his chest.

I shut my eyes, trying to focus my mind on something that might anchor me to reality. When I opened them again, Tom was standing directly in front of me, white-faced and holding the knife in his hand.

I'd been suffering from mild obsessive–compulsive disorder for months – if not for years – but it became much worse after Sam came out of hospital. I'd started to clean the house constantly, scrubbing and bleaching and vacuuming as though our lives depended on it – which, in fact, I believed they did. At least, I was haunted by the fear that if Sam touched something that wasn't clinically clean, he might become ill again – and it was my responsibility to prevent that happening.

I got through bottle after bottle of bleach. But when I looked at the surface of a just-cleaned table or the worktop in the kitchen, I imagined I could still see germs – tiny, filthy, toxic bacteria that were already multiplying into lethal colonies that could kill my son. So I'd scrub and clean everything again and I'd often get up in the night – some nights as many as 15 times – to vacuum the entire house. The sound of the vacuum cleaner would wake Sam up and he'd cry, and Tom would plead with me to stop. But I couldn't; I simply had no control over what I was doing. And the more exhausted I became, the more delusional I was.

One evening, before Tom was home from work, I started to get Sam ready for his nightly bath-time ritual. While the water was running into the bathtub, I peeled off his clothes, dropped them into the laundry basket on the landing outside the bathroom door and lifted him into his bath seat. He'd become almost too big and too mobile to sit in the seat any more, but he loved it and he was laughing excitedly as I man-oeuvred his legs into the space on either side of the central strut. Sam's enjoyment was infectious and for a moment I laughed too. Then I knelt on the floor beside the bath and handed him his carefully disinfected plastic dolphin.

Suddenly, I felt a familiar rush of anxiety and an image of one of the worktops in the kitchen flashed into my mind. I'd already scrubbed it with bleach half a dozen times since giving Sam his tea. But my need to clean and clean and then clean again was a compulsion that had nothing to do with rational thought. As soon as it started, I'd begin to sweat, my heart would beat so quickly it hurt, and I'd feel as though something was constricting my windpipe so that I couldn't breathe.

It was like a terrible, panicky fear that grew inside me until it blotted out everything else and became the only thing in the world that mattered. I gripped the side of the bath and tried to ignore it. But it was just a couple of seconds before I stood up and almost ran out of the bathroom, no longer aware of Sam splashing bathwater as he kicked his legs and gurgled with contentment.

In the kitchen, I took a new scouring pad out of the packet in the cupboard, poured bleach on to it and began to rub it, backwards and forwards, across the spotlessly clean work surface until the panic subsided enough to allow me to breathe again. And that's when I remembered Sam.

I called out to reassure him as I ran up the stairs, and then I stood in the doorway of the bathroom staring at the empty bath seat, not able to take in what I was looking at. Sam was lying face down in the water, but it was a few seconds before I managed to focus on his limp body. I screamed and lunged towards him, grabbing his arms and dragging him out of the bath while I shouted his name over and over again. I threw myself down on the floor and held him tightly against my chest, and then lay him across my knees, put my hands on his shoulders and gave his little body a firm shake.

Suddenly, he spluttered and struggled and began to cry. And, at that moment, I realised just how close I'd come to being responsible for the death of the one thing I loved more than anything else in the world; and I knew that I was really ill.

I wrapped Sam in a towel and held him on my knee while I phoned Tom at work and said, 'I nearly let Sam drown in the bath. I can't cope anymore. You've got to come home. I need you to help me.'

The next day, Tom rang the social worker who was already involved in monitoring things for Sam's sake. He told her what had happened and she said she'd come and see me as soon as she could during the day. Tom didn't go to work and, later that morning when a friend came to visit with her baby, we sat in the living room while the baby lay in her car seat and Sam played on the floor beside her.

I Remember, Daddy

The next thing I was aware of was being curled up in a ball in the corner of the room and looking up into the concerned face of my doctor. I had no memory of what had happened, but apparently I'd suddenly begun to sob hysterically and had run into the kitchen, snatched a knife from the drawer and tried to stab Tom again. I'd been shouting at him and calling him 'Dad' and then I'd thrown myself down on the floor and begun to babble wildly in the voice of a little girl.

The doctor tried to persuade me to go to hospital, but I refused, and eventually it was agreed that I could stay at home as long as I wasn't left alone with Sam, took the medication I was prescribed and spent every weekday at a day hospital. Sam was put on the Child Protection Register and Tom dropped him off at the house of a foster carer on his way to work every morning and picked him up on his way home in the evening. Tom's parents were upset about the arrangement, because they wanted to look after Sam themselves. But I was afraid that if he didn't come home every night, I'd rarely see him and then, after a while, he'd settle with his grandparents and wouldn't recognise me any more.

Over the next few months, I made slow, sometimes erratic, progress and there were many days when I doubted whether I'd ever be well again.

I felt proud of myself when I was finally allowed to take Sam to the foster carer's house in the mornings and pick him up in the afternoons, just before Tom got home from work. After that, Sam gradually began to spend less time with the foster carer and more time at home with me, until, when he was two, he started going to a nursery.

The things I had been – and still was – remembering about my father's sexual abuse and about the way he'd used me for the perverted, disgusting entertainment of his friends were too much for my mind to cope with. Although I listened to the psychiatrist's rational explanations about why I felt the way I did, and to what he told me about all those things having happened *to* me, and how I was a young child at the time and they weren't in any way my fault, I couldn't really absorb what he was saying. And, until my mind could accept it, it couldn't begin to repair the damage that had been done to me in so many ways.

I tried to be 'normal' and to think 'normal' thoughts. But, over the years, all the connections and ideas that had formed in my mind had been *ab*normal and, as they were the only connections and ideas I'd ever had, it felt as though I'd been left with no basis for making sense of anything. It was as if there were tens of thousands of tangled, cut wires hanging in useless confusion inside my head, and I had to start the seemingly impossible task of examining each one and trying to find and then link it to its correct counterpart. So I suppose it wasn't really surprising that every so often everything degenerated again into a crazy mess of disconnected chaos.

For Tom, the burden of all the worry must have been phenomenal and for a long time, when I was very ill, we couldn't have managed without all the help and support we were given. I was seeing the psychiatrist regularly, and eventually I began to feel as though I was starting to make progress on the difficult and often very distressing journey from despair to recovery.

There were still days when I slipped backwards, though, such as the day when I went on the bus with Sam to a supermarket just outside town. Although it wasn't very far away as the crow flies from where we lived, the bus went all around the houses on what began to seem like an endless route. I started to feel trapped and panicky, but I kept taking deep breaths and looking out of the window for things I could point out to show Sam, and finally we arrived at our stop.

As I carried Sam towards the supermarket, the light-headedness I was already experiencing got worse. Everything around me seemed unreal, as though I was on the outside of my life, watching myself through a window or acting on a stage. I stood still for a moment, trying to force myself to breathe slowly and waiting for my heartbeat to return to normal. Then I carried Sam into the glass-walled lobby of the store and pulled a trolley from the end of one of the long, interlinked rows, smiling at an elderly woman who stopped to help me. Sam's feet dug into the tops of my legs as he reached out excitedly towards the trolley. I held his arms to steady him as he stood on the red plastic flap of the child seat and then guided his chubby little legs through the holes until he was sitting down.

As I pushed the trolley towards the open inner door of the supermarket, an image flashed into my mind: Sam was floating, face upwards, in the bath, his eyes open and staring, while my father stood beside him, calmly removing his own clothes. I stopped beside the racks of magazines and untidy piles of newspapers, wiped the sweat from my hands on to my jeans, and then turned and walked out through the door without a backward glance.

It was almost like a blackout. I didn't plan to do it, or even realise what I'd done, and I don't know what I was thinking at the time – if anything. But when some-one found me a little while later in the staff area at the back of the shop, I was deeply distressed and in the midst of a panic attack.

I Remember, Daddy

Someone had already found Sam, apparently abandoned and all alone by the magazines, but still smiling cheerfully at everyone who came in through the doors. So it wasn't long before they put two and two together and realised we were connected. When he was finally able to get some sense out of me, the manager of the supermarket phoned Tom at work and he came to pick us up and take us home.

I don't know what came over me on that day, or on any of the other days when I abruptly became unable to cope. Sam was never a moment's trouble; he was the most good-natured, easily contented child anyone was ever blessed with, and I loved him with all my heart. So my reason for abandoning him and walking away had nothing to do with him. Something had triggered a memory, and once I started to panic, I was totally incapable of rational thought.

I'd sometimes wake up in the morning and it would slowly dawn on me that I felt all right. I'd lie in bed thinking, 'This is fine. I can do this,' and decide to go out somewhere. But when I got there, it would suddenly seem too much to cope with. I'd look around me at all the people behaving normally – talking to each other, pushing children in prams and buggies, and walking in and out of shops – and my heart would begin to pound. Within seconds, I'd be soaked in sweat, my whole body would be shaking and I'd feel a tight sensation across my chest that made me struggle to breathe. I'd think I was suffocating, that I was about to have a heart attack or lose my mind completely in the middle of the shopping centre, or wherever else I happened to be when the fear and terrible dread overwhelmed me.

There aren't really words to describe the way it feels to have a panic attack, or what it's like to live constantly with the anxiety of never knowing when it's going to happen. It didn't matter how much sleep I had, I was tired all the time. And what was even worse than the exhaustion was the fear: I was scared of what was happening to me and of never being able to cope again, and I was scared of being a mother to Sam.

Although I loved Sam, I didn't feel the way I imagined a mother should feel. It was as though I was watching him from a distance and he wasn't really connected to me. In fact, everything about my life was surreal. Sam was mine, and yet he didn't seem like mine; I loved him, but I was numb. I had no feelings about myself, so how could I feel anything for anyone else, even my own child? I was an adult woman, the mother of a little boy, and yet in my head I was a child myself, sometimes cowering, terrified, in the corner of a room, watching in case my father walked through an open door.

I Remember, Daddy

Perhaps the daze I was living in was caused by the medication I was taking, at least in part. Some of the drugs were supposed to help calm the chaotic perpetual motion in my mind and blot out the voices and memories that were constantly assailing my senses. So it would hardly have been surprising if they'd blurred not just the past but the present, too.

When Sam was two years old, we finally lost our house. For months, Tom had juggled his roles as father of a young son, husband of a crazy wife and sole provider. But it had been clear for some time that we wouldn't be able to go on paying the mortgage.

When the house was sold, we moved into a housing-association house in quite a nice part of town, and at last some of the pressure was lifted off Tom's shoulders. We were lucky, too, that his parents, brothers and sisters were so good to us and, particularly, to Sam; I don't know how we'd have managed without them.

Gradually, though, as the months passed, the medication that sometimes made me feel so detached from life began to stabilise the wild pitching and rolling of my mind, and eventually I was well enough to be able to go to night school to study human resource management. I couldn't drive, so it meant travelling an hour each way on the bus twice a week. But it was well worth the effort, because each bus journey seemed like a visible sign of the progress I was making. I was proud of myself – for the first time that I could remember: not only could I travel to college and back on my own without succumbing to panic attacks, I could also absorb and understand everything I was being taught.

I really did begin to feel as though I might one day live a normal life. Although I knew I could never close the lid on the Pandora's box that had been opened, releasing horrific memories of my child-hood, perhaps I *could* learn to see those memories as belonging to the past and, in time, be able to live with them.

Even when I was in hospital, I hadn't told my mother what I was remembering. But I decided that the time had come when she needed to know, if only so that she could understand what was wrong with me. I knew that it would be a very upsetting discussion, for both of us, and I thought that if we were in a public place, we'd be forced to control our emotions. So I asked her to meet me in a café in town.

We sat together at a table for two in an alcove at one side of the main room, drinking our coffee, and even-tually my mother said, 'So … What is it you wanted to tell me? I must say, I've been feeling a bit nervous since you phoned.'

I Remember, Daddy

'I wanted to tell you what's really wrong with me,' I told her, taking a deep breath and clasping my hands together tightly on the white damask tablecloth. 'I mean, what it is that's made me ill.'

My mother reached out a hand towards mine across the table and said, 'I know you've never really been happy. Not since you were a little girl. But the way you were after Sam was born was something completely different. I did wonder if it was just post-natal depression or if something else had happened to make you so ill.'

'Dad abused me,' I told her, blurting out the words in an angry whisper. 'He did it for years, from the time I was about two years old. But I'd forgotten until Sam was born.'

'Abused you?' My mother withdrew her hand and began searching through her handbag, which was something she often did when she was distressed. After a moment, she looked up at me again and asked, 'What do you mean "abused you"? He abused us all. Surely you hadn't forgotten his rages and the way he used to …'

'*Sexually* abused me,' I interrupted her. 'He did it to me, and his friends did it to me too.' I named a couple of my father's friends and for a moment I thought my mother was going to pass out.

The shock on her face was clearly genuine, and so were the fat tears that rolled slowly down her cheeks as the true horror of realisation and understanding began to dawn on her.

'My God! Oh my God,' she kept whispering, and then, eventually, 'It makes sense. I never knew. Oh Katie, you have to believe me. I never knew. I'd have killed him with my own bare hands if I'd even suspected he'd laid a hand on you in that way. The baths ... the naps ... Oh my God!'

And I felt bad for her, because I know that guilt is a terrible thing to have to live with.

Thirteen

Completing my course at college gave me a huge boost. I felt proud of myself, and even prouder when I applied for and was offered a job in the human resources department of a local company. Sadly, though, things between Tom and me weren't going so well, and we separated not longer after I started work.

We'd known so little about each other and we'd been together for such a short time when I became pregnant with Sam that it was surprising we'd made it as far as we had. It must have been really hard for Tom: within 18 months of our meeting and falling in love, I'd gone from apparent chirpy confidence to extreme mental illness, and his whole life had changed virtually overnight. Not only did he have a baby son and all the responsibilities that normally come with being a father, but he also had a very sick partner who needed constant care and attention, as well as never-ending worries about money. When I first became ill and was no longer able to work, he'd had to carry alone the financial burden of feeding, clothing and caring for three people and of trying to pay a mortgage we'd barely been able to afford on both our incomes.

We'd never actually got married in the end, despite Tom's intentions that day when we went to see my father at Christmas, and I knew how lucky I'd been that Tom had stuck by me when I was so ill. I was hugely grateful to his parents too, because, without the help and support they gave us, Sam would have been taken into care – and that would have been both terrible for Sam and an additional source of guilt for me that I don't think I could have lived with.

However, when I was well enough to work again and was coping better than I'd done for three or four years, Tom felt able to move on. It was one of the saddest days of my life when we went our separate ways, although we stayed friends and I knew I could rely on him to help me when things went wrong.

Even when I was well enough to work, I still had to take medication – and I remained dependent on it for the next 20 years. So, although I could hardly bear to think about it, it was clear to Tom and to me that Sam would be better off living with his father.

I Remember, Daddy

I sometimes felt as though I was swimming in the sea, trying to keep my eyes fixed on a horizon I couldn't really see and my head above water, and every wave that washed over me made me start to panic. Then, every so often, a really big wave would come along, my heart would start to race and I'd thrash about so wildly that, instead of saving myself from drowning, I'd actually make things much worse. I didn't want Sam to have to live like that too, buffeted and made anxious by every wave that *I* encountered. The only thing that really mattered was what was best for him, and in my heart I knew he needed to be with Tom. I couldn't look after him properly on my own; but if he lived with Tom, he'd always be safe and well cared for and I'd be able to see him whenever I wanted to, or if ever he needed me.

It was the hardest decision I've ever had to make. I cried myself to sleep night after night as I tried to come to terms with it, and I was full of hatred for my father for having done things to me when I was a little girl that made me unfit as an adult to look after my own child.

Sam was always pleased to see me, although it was clear that he was very happy living with Tom, and for a while everything seemed to be okay. The demons in my mind were apparently under control and I was feeling better than I'd done for a long time. I was really enjoying my job, and enjoying the thought that I was leading a 'normal' life again. At the weekends, I often went out with my friend Jenny and sometimes we'd run into a friend of my father or even my father himself.

Whenever we did meet my father, he'd chat up Jenny in a way that infuriated and disgusted me. Quite apart from the fact that he was more than twice her age, he knew that I'd been remembering things about my childhood, and if he'd stopped to think about it – which he probably didn't bother to do, as he was self-engrossed as well as thick-skinned – he'd have realised that Jenny must have known about at least some of those things. Perhaps he simply didn't care.

A couple of times on our nights out on the town, I bumped into a woman called Irene, who I sometimes used to see when I was in my teens at a pub frequented by my father and some of his work colleagues. I'd always thought Irene was a strange woman. She had a very pronounced squint in one eye and used to wear men's suits, and I'd assumed she was a lesbian. So I was particularly surprised when someone told me one day that she was pregnant.

I barely knew her, though, and I didn't think any more about it, until I was in a pub one evening and saw a friend of hers who said, 'Did you hear Irene had her baby? You do know it's your father's child, don't you?' I almost laughed out loud. Although I could easily accept that I might have been wrong about Irene's sexual identity, I knew that my father's choice of sexual partners tended to be teenage girls and attractive young women in their twenties. So I dismissed the claim as nonsense and forgot about it.

Then, one day, after hearing nothing from my father for months, I had a phone call from him.

'That bitch Irene is trying to take me for maintenance,' he shouted as soon as I picked up the telephone.

'I'm fine thank you, Dad,' I answered. 'And how are you?'

He ignored me and bellowed, 'Get that cow off my back. Or you'll get nothing.'

My irritation at his complete indifference to everything and everyone except himself and his own problems made me bold and I said, 'Well, that's not really much of an incentive, because I don't get anything anyway.'

'I'm warning you.' I could tell he was trying to control his fury and I began to enjoy his frustration – being bullied down a telephone line was quite a different thing from being shouted at face to face. 'I've got enough to deal with without this,' he snapped. 'She's *your* friend. Get her off my back.'

I laughed. 'I don't know why you say that,' I told him. 'I barely know her. She's not my friend at all. But it does sound as though she's been yours! If it *is* your child, pay for it.' And I put the phone down.

Then I sat for a while, half-expecting it to ring again, waiting for my body to stop shaking and trying to absorb the extraordinary new sensation of having answered my father back. I don't know what had possessed me. Perhaps it was just the realisation that I'd had so many really serious problems over the last few years, which had almost exclusively been caused by the unforgivable things my father had done to me when I was a child, and he hadn't cared or tried to do anything to help me. So his stupid, self-induced problems – which weren't *real* problems at all – just seemed like self-important melo-drama. It was nice to feel as though I'd been able to frus-trate him though, and that I'd dared to argue with him, even if it had been for just a few moments.

I heard later that Irene's child *was* proved to be my father's. Irene took him to court and he was ordered to pay maintenance for the child's support. Apparently, though, he swore she'd never get a penny, despite the court order, and I never did find out whether she did. I hope so. The money aside, however, she was lucky that my father didn't want to be involved with her child, because he caused nothing but harm to the chil-dren he did have contact with.

I met Irene's child, my little half-sister, a few years later, when she was about seven years old. But the thought of keeping in touch with her when our only real connection was my father – who I didn't want to be connected with in *any* way – was too painful, and I never saw her again.

In fact, from what I was told subsequently, we both had quite a few half-brothers and half-sisters. I don't know if that's true, although I can believe that it is, because my father had a very casual attitude towards sex – anything goes and the kinkier the better – and a very large number of sexual partners over the years.

There were often porn films running at his house when I visited him as a young teenager, and I'd sometimes see a flash as a photograph was taken of me when I was in bed with his friends as a little girl, although I didn't realise what was happening until much later. However, it seems that I wasn't the only one who was having my picture taken.

Before I was with Tom and had Sam, I was at my father's house one day. He was at work, Gillian had just popped out to the shops and I was cold – my father didn't believe in spending money on heating the house when he wasn't there – so I decided to look in the bedroom to see if I could find one of Gillian's sweaters to borrow.

It seemed like a reasonable enough thing to do when I thought of it. But, as I opened the bedroom door, I began to feel uncomfortable. It was before I'd started remembering that my father had sexually abused me, so I couldn't think why there was sweat on the palms of my hands and why my heart had begun to beat so fast. I decided it was probably just the thought of being in my father's bedroom, invading the inner sanctum where he and Gillian did things together that no one would ever want to try to imagine.

I laughed at myself, wiped my hands on my skirt and pulled open a drawer. Suddenly, it felt as though I was snooping, and I found that once I started, I couldn't stop. I looked in a couple of drawers in the polished-oak chest and then pulled open one of the small, half-width drawers at the top. It was full of photographs, all jumbled together in an untidy heap. I picked up a few, holding them on my open palm as I turned them round slowly with the fingers of my other hand and tried to work out what they were. And then I almost threw them back into the drawer as a feeling of sick disgust shot through me like a pain and I realised that all the photographs were of men, women, young girls and boys engaged in horrible, lewd sexual acts.

I slammed the drawer shut, automatically reaching out a hand to steady a vase that wobbled precariously on top of the chest. I kept swallowing, trying to get rid of the sharp, burning sensation at the back of my throat, and then, with the sound of my heart thumping loudly in my ears, I ran out of the room, having completely forgotten about my intention of searching for a sweater.

However hard I tried, I never managed to block out from my mind the images I saw that day.

Later, when the memories of being sexually abused as a child had begun to return, I wished I'd scooped up a handful of the photographs and taken them with me, as evidence of the fact that my father was not at all the man he might appear to be. I thought that no one would ever believe me if I told them the truth about him. And then, a few years after Tom and I split up, it began to appear as though I wasn't the only one who knew more about my father than he'd have wanted anyone to know.

I was at work one morning when the phone rang and a man's voice I didn't recognise said, 'Is that Katie Matthews?'

'Yes, this is Katie,' I answered.

'Katie Matthews, daughter of Harold Matthews?' he persisted.

There was something about his tone and the emphatic way he said my father's name that made me feel uneasy. I hadn't seen my father for some time and my first thought was that this man was phoning me to tell me he'd died – and I didn't know how I felt about that.

'Who is this?' I asked.

'I'm a journalist,' the man answered, and he said his name and the name of the newspaper he worked for. 'I was hoping you might answer some questions about your father.'

'Why? What sort of questions?' I tried not to sound as panic-stricken as I felt.

'Questions about the accusations that have been made against him of being a modern-day slum land-lord,' the man said, and then added as if it was an afterthought, 'Oh, and about his liking for having sex with underage girls and young boys.'

His tone was incongruously chatty, and I gave a bark of laughter, which I hurriedly tried to cover up by coughing and clearing my throat.

'Young boys?' I repeated incredulously, although in reality nothing would have surprised me about my father when it came to sex, because I knew he was happy to try anything and everything, at least once.

'Ah, so you're surprised to hear about the boys, but not about the accusations that he's had sex with under-age girls.' The journalist made it sound as though I'd made a statement rather than asked a question, and I began to feel nervous as I realised that by saying anything at all, I was giving him the opportunity to 'quote' me.

'There's going to be an article in the paper,' he continued, in a friendly, confiding sort of tone. 'So I just wanted to give you the chance to comment ahead of time, in case there was anything you wanted to say in defence of your father – or otherwise.'

It was clear that what he was really hoping for was for me to say something 'otherwise'. But it wasn't the journalist I was afraid of; it was my father.

'I didn't say that I was surprised about the boys. I ... What I mean is ... Look, I'm sorry, I don't have anything to say,' I told him, and I could still hear the metallic squawking of his voice as I replaced the telephone receiver on my desk.

I sat for a moment with my arms crossed in front of me in a subconscious gesture of self-protection. I felt sick and my whole body was shaking, but I wasn't sure precisely which aspect of what had just happened was making me feel so ill.

For a while, there were stories in the media, but I knew that however terrible the revelations that were made about my father, he wasn't ashamed or remorseful about a single one of all the dreadful things he'd done, including almost destroying the life of his own daughter. And despite the media interest in him, I'm sure he still felt invincible, because he sometimes told me, 'If I ever go down, I'll be taking a lot of people with me. As I've always said, I plan to have the last laugh.'

I was still taking medication to enable me to function more or less normally. Sometimes I was well and sometimes I had to have time off work and go through yet another series of appointments with my psychiatrist. I *wanted* to leave the past behind me and get on with my life, but there was so much to try to come to terms with and so much I still couldn't even begin to understand.

Throughout most of my childhood, my father had bullied, beaten and sexually abused me and, perhaps worse than that – although it's difficult to draw up a scale of 'bad, worse and worst' in relation to a man's sexual abuse of his own daughter – he'd encouraged his friends to abuse me too. None of the people who knew him could ever have said that he wasn't a great host at the many parties he threw: at how many other parties would you be offered not only cigars, drugs and the best champagne, which flowed like water, but also the chance to have sex with your host's little girl?

By the time I was in my early teens and my mind had begun to lock away the appalling memories it couldn't process or make sense of, I felt worthless, dirty and unlovable – and I didn't know why. Once I'd forgotten the aspects of my childhood that had been most important in moulding the person I was becoming, I couldn't understand why I was so unhappy and so full of undirected anger and sometimes hatred – both of myself and of anyone who bullied or treated me badly. I just assumed there was something wrong with me and that, as my father had told me for as long as I could remember, *everything* was my fault.

Then, as the memories began to return, it was as though my life had been shattered into pieces, like a mirror smashed with a hammer. I managed to reassemble part of it, but I was still searching frantically in the dark for the tiny shards of glass that would make the mirror whole again and that would enable me to see a clear reflected image of myself. Every time I saw my father – which wasn't often during that period of my life – I'd feel an anger and resentment towards him that I didn't fully understand. Somehow, though, I always knew that he was the person who'd wielded the hammer and smashed the mirror in the first place.

Eventually, I decided to write a letter to him, telling him about the things I'd been remembering and demanding an explanation for what he'd done to me. I don't know what I thought he was going to say, and whether I really believed that he might admit to the things he'd done – particularly because I knew that he was a supremely arrogant man who never apologised or explained himself to anyone. But I wrote the letter anyway, and gave it to someone who I knew was meeting my father the next day for a meal at a restaurant.

I didn't tell the bearer of my letter what was written in it and, apparently, when he handed it over, my father read it without a word. Then he folded it up again, replaced it in its envelope, tucked it into the inside pocket of his jacket and said, in a wounded, incredulous tone, 'Well, I can't believe it. She called me a bully. I'm not a bully!'

It was the one thing he'd taken exception to. I'd catalogued his sexual abuse of me and asked him, 'What sort of man takes a child into his bath, pushes her head under the water and makes her do what you used to make me do to you? And what sort of man takes his daughter into his bed and does the things you used to do to me?' But none of the accusations that he was a paedophile who'd sexually abused and prostituted his own young daughter seemed to have upset him. What had really annoyed him and struck him as being unfair was the claim that he was a bully!

Looking back now, I realise I was very ill when I wrote that letter to my father, and although everything I accused him of was perfectly true, most of what I'd written probably sounded pretty crazy. He answered it anyway, though – and in writing, which was a very unusual thing for my father to do, because he never wrote letters. He had too much to hide, both in his personal and business lives, and he was always careful not to leave a paper trail of any sort. Even in the letter he *did* write to me, he was too clever to admit to anything. It was full of phrases like, 'If you want to talk to me about things that have happened in your life, just contact me' and 'I know your mother put lots of ideas into your head.'

I think he must have been a bit nervous, however, because he could just have ignored the letter altogether – like he ignored everything else he didn't want to have to deal with. It was obvious that he wanted me to contact him so that we could talk. But part of his job – which he did so well, with such acclaimed success – was to twist and spin and disguise reality to make things appear to be different from the way they actually were. I'd heard him out-talk and out-smart people with far sharper wits than I had, and without the debilitating, destructive emotional baggage that I was carrying. So talking to him face to face was something I was never going to try to do.

Fourteen

After Tom and I split up, it took me a long time to pay off my share of the debts and to get back on my feet financially. I tried to rebuild a life for myself, both for my own sake and so that Sam wouldn't grow up feeling that his mother lived on the edge of society, defined by her illness and her inability to cope. I just kept plodding on, making sometimes painfully slow progress towards achieving my aim of 'being normal'.

It was as though there was an invisible line between the well side of me and the ill side, and I was trying to traverse along it, like a tightrope walker, balancing precariously as I edged my way, one careful step at a time. The tightrope constantly swayed beneath my feet, and sometimes I'd wobble and lean too far towards the ill side, and sometimes I'd fall and would have to struggle to climb back on to it again. Then I'd wait until the worst of the swaying stopped and I was steady enough to be able to continue my cautious progress – until the next time I missed my footing and fell again. The trouble was, though, that it took a huge amount of effort just to stay on the tightrope at all, and even when I seemed to be balanced and relatively safe, I knew that at some point not too far ahead, I'd fall again.

This time, though, I remained 'normal' long enough to be able to buy a small one-bedroom house and, for a while, things seemed to be going well. But then the tightrope swayed and I couldn't keep my balance, the cycle of illness started again and I had to give up my job, which meant that I didn't have enough money to pay my bills, and everything began to come crashing down around my ears once more.

When nothing else worked, drinking seemed to block out the images and silence the voices in my head – for a while, at least – and I'd begun to drink heavily. This time, though, not even alcohol succeeded in stopping the endless, exhausting whirring round and round of thoughts in my mind. I was weary of struggling repeatedly to get back on my feet; there didn't seem to be any point in it, particularly when I knew that it was only a matter of time before I'd be right back where I started. And then I began to hear one clear voice in my head saying, 'Why not just give up?'

During the periods when I was ill, I'd sometimes be almost consumed by hatred for my father, and I'd sit hugging my knees to my chest and thinking about him. I had friends whose fathers had always done everything they could to make their sons' and daughters' lives easier for them, whereas my father had taken every imaginable and unimaginable step to ensure that *my* life would be as difficult as it could possibly be.

One night, after drinking a couple of bottles of wine and finding they'd done nothing to blot out the dark thoughts that stopped me sleeping, I took an overdose – a cocktail of paracetamol and the anti-psychotic medication I was supposed to take but that I'd been hoarding for several days. I didn't really intend to kill myself; I just wanted to sleep. But maybe it was because I was afraid I might have taken too many tablets and would die all alone and not be found for days that I phoned Tom.

Tom and I had been apart for a few years, although we saw each other regularly when I went to pick up Sam or dropped him at home again. In the early days after we separated, I used to phone Tom when I was low, and he'd talk to me and do what he could to help me. However, he had a fiancée by this time, and she was asleep in the bed beside him when I phoned.

I Remember, Daddy

'Jesus Christ, Katie.' Tom's voice was muffled by sleep. 'What time is it?'

He was quiet for a moment and I could imagine him reaching out his hand to pick up his watch from the table beside the bed.

'I just wanted to talk to someone,' I told him, wiping tears on to the sleeve of my dressing-gown.

'Well, I don't want to talk to you. Not now. Not at this time of night,' Tom said in an angry whisper. 'Just go to bed and go to sleep. And *don't* phone me at 3 in the morning again.'

There was a click as he replaced the receiver, and I sat for a while, holding the phone on my lap. The next thing I knew, I was in an ambulance and my brother Ian was sitting beside me.

Ian stayed at the hospital until I'd stopped being sick and they'd found me a bed and admitted me for what remained of the night. Then he stood looking down at me and said, 'Tom phoned me. You were unconscious by the time I got to the house. So I had to break down the door to get in.' He shrugged as he added, 'Sorry.'

'You know why I did it, don't you?' I asked him. 'You know what Dad did …'

Ian took a step backwards away from the bed and said, 'I don't want to talk about our childhood – ever. It's in the past, Katie. It isn't relevant to anything any more.'

'But it's relevant to me,' I told him. I tried to lift my head from the pillow to look at him, but it felt as though someone had removed all the muscles in my neck. 'It affects every minute of every single day of my life. I wish I could forget it. I wish it hadn't ever happened and I wish I'd never remembered it. But …'

'I'm sorry, Katie.' Ian pushed his hands into the pockets of his jacket and hunched his shoulders as though against an imaginary wind. 'I've got to go. Take care of yourself. It isn't the answer you know – taking an overdose.'

And then he left, and a few seconds later I drifted at last into a deep sleep.

I'd never been very close to my brother. He was married by that time and had a young child, but we rarely had much contact. However, he must have realised that I was approaching rock bottom and he apparently told my father, 'We're going to lose Katie one of these days. She self-harms, she's taken an overdose and tried to kill herself, and she's desperate for money so that she doesn't lose her home again.'

As a result – and much to my amazement – my father agreed to make my mortgage payments until I could get back on my feet. Nothing my father did was ever simple and straightforward, though, and giving me the money proved to be a characteristically complicated process. Every month, he would give the cash to Gillian – who, by this time, had become the third Mrs Matthews – and she'd put it in an envelope, write my name on it and give it to my brother's wife, who would then give it to me. At least, that's what happened for three months, until my father lost interest and the envelopes stopped arriving.

When my next mortgage payment became due and' I didn't hear anything from my brother or his wife, I waited a few days and then phoned my father.

'I didn't get the money for my mortgage this month,' I told him.

I hated having to ask him for anything – although, God knows, he owed me more than he could ever repay. So the feeling that I was begging him for a favour made me angry and, without waiting for him to answer, I shouted, 'Couldn't you be a proper father, just once? Couldn't you help me when I need help? I'm going to lose my house.'

I should have known that I was wasting my time trying to appeal to any sense he might have of paternal duty. Like so many things that didn't directly provide him with amusement and some sort of personally positive payback, the idea of 'being a father' to me held absolutely no interest for him at all. Although he'd helped me for a while because my brother had asked him to, in reality he was completely indifferent to my problems. So he didn't send me any more money, and I lost my house.

I seemed to be trapped in a vicious circle that often made it impossible to see any point in trying to struggle on. I'd be ill and have to give up work, and then I'd get (reasonably) well again, so I'd get another job and be able to pay for somewhere decent to live; then I'd get ill again and have to give up work … However much I tried, there didn't seem to be any way of breaking out of the cycle, or any realistic possibility that I might one day be able to live a normal life.

For years, I'd lived with a deep sense of despair I hadn't understood, until I'd been ill for the first time, after Sam was born, and the illness had triggered memories that had provided an explanation for the way I'd always felt. The trouble was, though, that those memories, once recalled, could never be forgotten again. Which meant that, in some ways, all that had really happened was that I'd swapped unhappiness I didn't know the reasons for for unhappiness whose reasons were more awful than anything I could ever have imagined.

Sometimes, my father would get Gillian to phone me and tell me he wanted me to join them for a meal at their home or at a restaurant. Then I'd sit and watch him eating good food, drinking expensive champagne and telling funny stories that made everyone laugh. It was clear that his friends admired and even envied him; whereas I sometimes felt a hatred for him that was so intense it made my hands shake.

One day after I'd lost my house, I walked out of the front door of my rented flat, down the dingy communal staircase, and through town to the large, impressive Victorian building where my father worked. The man at the reception desk recognised me and said 'Good morning' as I walked past him and up the wide, curved staircase to the first floor. But instead of going directly to my father's office, I slipped, unnoticed, into the oak-panelled library.

The room was suffused with a golden-yellow light that threw sharply defined images of the tall arched windows on to the polished wooden floor. I sat down for a moment, perched on the edge of one of the overstuffed, high-backed leather armchairs, clutching my handbag to my chest and breathing in the smell of the old musty books that lined every wall. Then I took one deep breath, stood up and walked out of the library, along the red-carpeted corridor towards my father's office.

As I opened the door, his secretary looked up with a professionally friendly expression, which turned to surprise as she recognised me. She was older than all my father's previous secretaries – in mid-middle age, at least. Her hair was a mousy brown and she had a pronounced gap between her front teeth, which showed when she smiled, which she did again, although this time more warily, as she said, 'Hello dear.'

Her tone was briskly patronising, but perhaps she was just taken aback by the intrusion of the unexpected into her well-organised and well-ordered day.

'Are you looking for your father?' she asked, adding before I had a chance to answer, 'I'm afraid he isn't here at the moment. He'll be out at meetings all morning. He wasn't expecting you, was he?'

She turned the pages of a large leather-bound desk diary, as if searching for some missed note of my appointment, while at the same time managing to convey the fact that she was looking only in order to humour me, because nothing in her domain was ever missed.

'No. No, I was … I was just passing,' I told her. 'Never mind. I'll come back another time.'

I turned towards the door, fumbling with the handle in my haste to get out of the room before she tried to stop me, and then I fled back along the corridor, down the sweeping staircase and across the marble-floored lobby to the real world outside.

When I was at a safe distance from the building, I paused and looked over my shoulder to see if anyone was following me. Then I darted into a phone box, still clutching my handbag to my chest. I jabbed at the numbers on the phone with my index finger and listened as it rang twice, three times.

'Please be there; please pick up the phone,' I whispered into the receiver. And, at that moment, the ringing stopped and Jenny's voice said, 'Hello.'

'Jenny.' I began to cry silently.

'Hello. Who is this?' Jenny sounded irritated, but her tone quickly changed as she said, 'Katie? Is that you, Katie? Say something. Are you all right? What's happened? Speak to me, Katie.'

'Can you come and get me?' I said, in the voice of an unhappy child.

'What's the matter?' I could tell she was trying to sound calm. 'Has something happened? Where are you?'

'I'm near my father's office,' I told her. 'I'm in the phone box round the corner. I've … I've got a knife.' I sobbed one loud choking sob and tightened my grip on my handbag.

'Listen to me, Katie. Can you hear me?' Jenny spoke slowly, as if to a rather slow-witted – or very frightened – child.

'Yes,' I whispered.

'I want you to stay exactly where you are. Can you do that? Don't go anywhere. Do you understand, Katie? Promise me you'll wait at the phone box until I get there.' She paused and then said again, 'Promise me, Katie.'

'I promise,' I said, and immediately the phone line went dead.

I don't know how long I waited in the phone box, crouched on the floor with my handbag still pressed against my chest, until Jenny came and found me and took me home to her house.

She made me lie on the sofa, covered me with a blanket and told me to try to sleep. And neither of us mentioned what we both knew: that if my father had been at his office that day, I'd have tried to kill him.

It wasn't the only occasion when I set out to kill my father. I was at Jenny's house for supper one evening when I suddenly jumped to my feet, knocking over my chair and stumbling against the table. I'd been feeling light-headed and detached all day, and although I was on heavy medication at the time, I'd been drinking, and while we were eating our meal, I'd begun to talk about my father.

Sometimes I'd become obsessed by him. It might be triggered by a casual comment or even a smell that evoked some half-formed memory, and then it would gradually escalate into a fixation, so that I could think of nothing else. It had started that evening, and Jenny and her husband Neil had tried repeatedly to head me off and change the subject. However, it was a process I simply couldn't stop once it had started, and it was already too late.

As I stood up from the table, Neil got to his feet too. But by the time he'd followed me into the kitchen, I'd already snatched up a carving knife, which I waved in front of me as I swung round to face him.

'I want to go to my father's house,' I told Neil.

He took a cautious backward step away from me and put his hands out, palm downwards, in a placating gesture.

'Come on, Katie,' he said. 'Put the knife down. You know you don't really want to hurt anyone, not even your father. It's just not worth it.'

'I don't care!' I shouted, like an angry child. 'I'm going to kill him. He's ruined my life and taken everything away from me. I've got nothing, while he sits there in his big house, having a great time and being admired by everyone for being so wonderful and so clever. If I can't have my life back, then he doesn't deserve to have one either.'

'Katie, please. Put the knife down.' Jenny was standing in the kitchen doorway behind Neil.

I ignored her and shouted at Neil, 'Take me to my father's house.' Then I stepped towards him, the knife held out in front of me.

'Okay. Okay.' Neil reached around the side of me with exaggeratedly slow care to pick up his car keys from the kitchen work surface and, as he did so, I caught a glimpse of Jenny's anxious face behind him.

As soon as we pulled up outside my father's house, I knew he wasn't there. There was no car in the driveway and the large outer double doors were shut, which only ever happened when the house was locked up and empty. Neil turned the car around and took me back to stay the night with him and Jenny, and it was only some time later that I realised he'd never have let me do anything to my father anyway. He'd driven me there because he was afraid that if he didn't, I'd find some other way to get there, or might turn the knife on myself instead, and because he was hoping – rightly, as it turned out – that if he could buy some time, it would give me the chance to calm down.

I think I was just searching for some way to do *something* that might make the torment stop. I'd been having counselling for years, since I'd first started to remember; but I was still having horrible nightmares. It seemed as though I'd always been afraid of the nighttime – as a child, when I used to hide in my wardrobe with a sheet over my head, praying that when my father opened the door he wouldn't see me; and then as an adult, too frightened to close my eyes because of the dreams, invoked by memories, that haunted my sleep.

After my parents divorced and the court ordered my father to pay maintenance, he'd declared himself bankrupt every time it had looked as though he was going to be forced to pay up, and he'd put almost everything he owned into someone else's name, latterly Gillian's. So, on paper at least, he appeared to have nothing of any value at all.

My mother hadn't ever pursued him for the money he'd been ordered to pay her. She knew that his determination not to pay was far stronger than her own desire to get from him the money she was due, and that she wouldn't be able to cope with the long, difficult battle it would involve. After I told her about how my father had abused me, however, she changed her mind. It was as though she felt that because she hadn't done anything to protect me at the time – although she hadn't known what was happening – she needed to act in some way and do something now. And, this time, she was absolutely firm in her resolve to fight for what was rightfully hers.

It must have been shortly after my father received a letter from my mother's lawyer informing him that she was taking him to court that he phoned me.

'You're not going to get a single penny out of me,' he shouted as soon as I picked up the receiver.

The unexpected sound of his voice sent a shudder through my body and my eyes snapped shut in an involuntary twitch. Then, for some reason, something made me press 'Record' on my answering machine.

'That bitch of a mother of yours is getting noth-ing. Do you hear me?' His voice had risen to a fren-zied scream. 'Nothing! No bloody court in the land is going to be able to make me give her any money. She can forget it. If she's got money to spend on lawyer's fees, she doesn't need anything from me. You're just the same, both of you: lazy and worthless. You think you can sponge off men and that we're here to provide you with money while you sit back and do fuck all.'

It was an accusation that was unfair on both counts: my father had been legally obliged to pay maintenance to my mother while I was a child, which he'd failed to do; and I'd never asked him for anything other than to help me keep my home during a period when I'd been too ill to work – with an illness that had been caused by what he'd done to me. I was upset, as I always was, by his nastiness and threats. But this time I felt a sense of satisfaction at the thought that I'd outsmarted him, because I had his rant on tape, as proof of what he was really like.

As the pendulum that ruled my life swung back towards 'normal' and I began to feel well again, I landed a good job selling advertising space for a maga-zine. I really enjoyed it. I liked the people I worked with and I was good at what I was doing, and it wasn't long before I was promoted. Then, one day, my father contacted me out of the blue – although, in fact, it was actually Gillian who phoned me.

'Your father wondered if you'd like to come up to the house for dinner,' she told me, trying, unsuccessfully, to make it sound like a casual suggestion, despite the fact that I hadn't seen my father for some months.

'Really? Why?'

Surprise and mild suspicion were evident in my voice, and Gillian sounded embarrassed as she said, 'Well, we've heard about how well you're doing in your new job and I think your father wanted to catch up on your news – and to see you, of course. We haven't seen you in ages.'

'Okay,' I said, and I think she could imagine the shrug that expressed my lack of enthusiasm at the prospect.

A few days later, I arrived at my father's house at the appointed hour and he greeted me, as he always did unless he was angry with me, by proffering a cheek for me to kiss. During dinner, he talked a lot of inconsequential rubbish that served only to deepen my bewilderment about why he'd asked me to come. My father had never in his whole life *wanted* to see me, and I knew he must have a reason this time for pretending that he did. There was something going on, although I couldn't put my finger on exactly what it was.

At one point during the evening, while Gillian was clearing away dirty plates from the dining table, my father leaned back in his chair, folded his hands in front of him and said, 'Now then, why don't you tell me all about your childhood.' Then he laughed a nasty, sneering laugh, as though he was daring me to say something.

'I don't want to go into that now,' I told him, swallowing the saliva that had filled my mouth and praying I wasn't actually going to vomit all over the table.

He laughed again, but he changed the subject, and we ate the rest of our meal and drank our wine while he held court, as he always did. Then, when we were eating our dessert, he asked me casually about some problems I'd had when I sold my house. When I'd bought the house, my lawyer hadn't picked up on the fact that it had quite extensive damp, so I'd ended up having to sell it at a loss, and then I'd become locked in a half-hearted battle with the lawyer about compensation.

'Don't worry about it,' my father said, flapping his napkin over the side of his chair. 'I'll get some of my legal friends on to it for you. They'll sort it out.'

'Yeah, thanks,' I said, not really taking much notice, because I knew that his offers of help rarely materialised.

'Well, it's time you were going home,' he said abruptly, dropping his napkin on to the table and pushing back his chair. 'Gillian's going to drive you, and I can see she's getting tired.'

I stood up and lifted my handbag from where I'd hooked it over the back of my chair.

'Oh, and before you go, just let me get a bit of paper.' He walked over to the oak dresser that stood against the wall on one side of the room, rummaged for a few moments through its top drawer and then said, 'Ah, here we are', before turning and sitting down again at the table.

He unscrewed the top of his pen, wrote something in his flamboyant hand, and then pushed the piece of paper across the table towards me and handed me his pen.

I read the words he'd written: 'I, Katherine Matthews'.

'Just sign your name and I'll fill in all the blah blah later,' he told me.

'Fill it in with what?' I asked him. 'I don't know what you mean. What is it?'

'I told you,' he said, waving his hand dismissively. 'I'll see what I can do about sorting out the problems with the lawyer – about the damp. I'll fill in all the legal jargon afterwards. All you need to do is write your signature and I can deal directly with your lawyer.' Then he laughed spitefully as he added, 'Have all the drugs affected your memory?'

'But, I don't …' I didn't know what to say. It wasn't like my father to take any interest at all in my problems. The only times he'd even pretended to do so were when he was showing off to other people about what a wonderful, generous father he was. But, each time, he'd failed to see his promises through, and his good intentions – if he'd ever actually had any – had evaporated as soon as his audience had gone. So, this time, something didn't seem right.

'We haven't got all night,' my father said. He smiled a quick smile to try to cover up the impatience in his voice and added, 'Poor old Gillian wants to get to her bed.' He looked across the table at Gillian with a lewd, suggestive grin and she lowered her eyes.

'Just sign there.' He jabbed at the piece of paper with his finger, and I wrote my name with his pen.

Instantly, before the ink had even dried on the page, he seemed to lose interest in the subject. Smoothing the paper with his hands, he said 'Goodbye' and then left the room.

Gillian tried to hide her discomfort under a false cheerfulness as she drove me home, and 20 minutes later I was closing the front door of my flat and wondering what my father was really up to.

Before Gillian had phoned and asked me to dinner, he hadn't contacted me for months. So I'd assumed that the real reason for his invitation had been because there was something he wanted to tell me, or, more likely, some information he wanted to prise out of me. But, as I went over the evening's conversations in my head, I couldn't think of anything that had been said that could have been of potential interest or importance to him. I decided he must just have wanted to find out about my new job at the magazine, so that he could assess whether there was any aspect of it that might prove useful – or potentially threatening – to him in some way. As usual, though, there was no point speculating about my father's real intentions for doing anything. Only time would tell.

Three weeks later, I phoned my solicitor and asked if my father had been in touch with him.

'Your father?' the solicitor said. 'No. Why would your father get in touch with me?'

'About the damp in the house,' I told him. 'Although, actually, it might not have been my father himself; I think he was going to get someone else – one of his legal people – to contact you to try to sort it all out.'

'I don't really understand what you mean.' The solicitor sounded bemused. 'I haven't heard anything from anyone about it.'

And that was that. My father never did step in to help me. So it looked as though the real reason he'd made me sign that blank piece of paper would remain a mystery.

Fifteen

Remembering had provided me with an explanation of why I'd always felt as though, if people really knew me, there was something about me they'd be horrified and disgusted by. It had been a feeling I couldn't understand, until the memories started to return and I realised why I'd always felt as though I was contaminated and somehow dirty. I suppose it was better in the long run actually to know what had made me feel that way, but knowing was also the reason I started to drink bleach.

The first time I did it, I drank just a couple of mouthfuls, in the hope that I might be able to cleanse myself and remove the dark, disgusting stain inside me. It tasted foul, and it burned my mouth and throat painfully as I swallowed it. That seemed like a good thing, though, because it was another way of self-harming; a new way to punish myself for … I didn't really know what.

It felt like pure acid as it flowed down my oesophagus and then as though burning fingers were gripping my stomach. I crouched on the floor, panting and waiting for the intensity of the pain to subside, and then I began to retch and vomit up blood. But despite the pain and the horrible raw feeling inside me, I had a sense of satisfaction as I imagined it flushing through my body, dissolving all the filth my father had put inside me.

After that first time, I drank mouthfuls of bleach at least once almost every week for about 18 months. Although swallowing it was agonising and I was frightened by the blood that instantly filled my mouth and later came out when I went to the toilet, it made me feel better – cleaner – for a little while, at least. The physical pain somehow seemed to release some of my mental pain, although the effect was always disappointingly short-lived, and the bleach caused permanent damage to my insides, for which I still have to take daily medication.

The first time I'd taken an overdose, I hadn't really intended to kill myself. But, one morning when I woke up, it was as though something inside me had died. Overnight, I seemed to have gone from weary to completely exhausted by the effort of constantly having to *try*, of always struggling and hoping that the future might be better, and I decided to end it, once and for all. For the last few weeks, I'd been spiralling down again into hopeless despair and I knew I couldn't go on pretending everything was all right.

I cried when I thought about never seeing Sam again. I knew, though, that he was happy living with his father, whereas I felt I had nothing to offer him and he'd be better off without me. I thought about my best friend Jenny too, and how she'd stood by me and supported me ever since we were at school together. And although I knew she'd be angry with me for what I was going to do, it never crossed my mind that it might cause her actual distress. Mentally, I was, quite literally, in a world of my own. When I was ill, I was totally self-centred; everything around me contracted down to just the things that affected me, making me incapable of imagining how other people might feel as a result of my actions, particularly if I killed myself.

That morning, I was convinced that taking my own life was the only way out of the miserable, never-ending battle I had to fight every single day. The images of what my father did to me when I was a child were always with me. There didn't seem to be anything I could do to block them out, although the medication helped, and sometimes the drinking too. Each time I

I Remember, Daddy

began to get a bit better and could imagine that, one day, I might be able to cope and move on with my life, something knocked me back again. On this occasion, I'd been having vivid flashbacks, which were pulling me deeper and deeper down into a dark pit of hopelessness, and I was convinced that I was dragging down with me the people I loved.

It's difficult to explain how the flashbacks – as well as all the other memories – affected me. It was partly their relentlessness that was so debilitating. Normally, if you look out of a window, you see what's there: houses, fields, trees … But wherever I looked I saw what was already in my head: my father leaning over me as I lay in bed, or crushing me with the weight of his body until I was gasping for breath, or pushing my head under the bathwater and holding it there until my lungs pressed against my ribcage.

When I was ill, those images were always there, wherever I looked and whatever I was doing. And so was my fear – often a non-specific, undirected fear that was sometimes so strong it almost paralysed me – and my sense of self-disgust. All the images and emotions tumbled around constantly in my head, like physical objects in a perpetually spinning washing machine. I wanted to make it stop, to shut out for ever all the things I didn't want to see or think about. And I didn't know how else to do it.

I'd been stockpiling tablets for weeks – mostly paracetamol and chlorpromazine, which were the antipsychotic pills I was supposed to take every day – and I went into the kitchen and started to swallow them, forcing them down, one by one, with sips of water. As I stood there, I could see my father leaning against the old butler's sink in the kitchen of the house we'd lived in when I was a child. He had a glass in his hand and one corner of his thin lips was raised in a cruel sneer. 'Useless', I heard him say. Then he threw back his head and roared with laughter.

The room turned slowly around me and I began to feel dizzy and sick. My father was right: I *was* useless; I was a worthless, bad person who did nothing for the people I loved except cause them pain. I deserved to die.

I reached out my hand towards the knife block on the work surface beside the small kitchen window and closed my fingers around the wooden handle of one of the knives, sliding it out of its slot and holding it for a moment in front of me. Then I began to make small cuts on the underside of my left arm, slashing and slicing at the skin to release some of the pain that was always inside me.

A sudden wave of nausea washed over me and I reached out my hand to steady myself against the kitchen table, and at that moment the doorbell rang.

I Remember, Daddy

I stumbled to the front door and pulled it open and my friend Debs gasped as she took a step backwards, her eyes wide with shock, and said, 'Jesus Christ, Katie! What are you doing?'

I followed the direction of her horrified stare and looked down at the knife that was still in my hand and at the blood trickling down my arm. And that's when I must have fainted.

When I came round, someone I didn't recognise was looking down at me and I heard a voice say, 'Ah, you're back with us. Come on now, love. Let's get you into the car.'

A few seconds later, I was slumped in the back of a police car as it sped through the busy city streets to the hospital.

When the wounds on my arm had been cleaned, I was given an injection and then transferred by ambulance to a locked ward in a psychiatric hospital, where I was sectioned. Although I hated the thought of being locked up again, I didn't resist. I'd tried to kill myself because I was useless, and so unhappy I couldn't bear to live through another day. And I'd failed – which simply proved just how useless I really was. So I thought I deserved whatever happened to me.

In reality, however, being locked up was even worse than I'd remembered. When you're as ill as I was, you're afraid of everything, and I felt incredibly vulnerable. It was as though all the thoughts and images in my mind were on scraps of paper that kept blowing away out of reach every time I tried to grasp hold of one. The one thing I *was* sure of, though, was that I couldn't trust anyone. I knew that everyone at the hospital was trying to get me to drop my guard – by giving me injections to 'calm me down' or by appearing to be kind and understanding – and that as soon I did, they'd … I didn't know what it was they were planning to do; I just knew that I must never relax.

I'd beg everyone – the nurses, my mother and any other visitors who came to see me – to get me out of there. 'Surely you can see that I shouldn't be here,' I'd plead with them, and I'd promise them anything if they'd help me to escape. Then I'd hate them when they all said, in the same nanny-ish voice, 'You need to be here, Katie. You're here for your own good, to help you get well again.' And my fear and anxiety would grow stronger, because I knew that they, too, were part of the plot to keep me there against my will.

My mother did seem to agree with me, however, and one day when she came to see me, she broke down and cried and – as she'd done once before, on the first occasion when I'd been in the psychiatric hospital – she told a nurse I shouldn't be there amongst all those crazy, sick people. And again I realised later that we were both wrong and that I did need to be in the hospital, because I was crazy and sick too.

It must have been horribly distressing for my mother to see me in that state, surrounded by patients who sometimes became angry and violent, but many of whom were no more deranged than I was. I didn't think about my mother's distress, though, or about anything outside myself. I was locked inside my own mind – and that was a very frightening place to be.

When it became clear that no one was going to help me get out of there, I started trying to run away. Just as I'd done before, during the six months I'd spent in hospital after Sam was born, I'd stand for hours near the locked door that divided the ward from the long corridor leading to the world outside, watching and waiting for the moment when I could escape. I'd got out of the hospital on a few occasions last time I was there, but I never did manage it this time. In the event, though, it didn't matter so much, because I wasn't there for very long.

The medication I'd been taking needed to be adjusted, and once they'd found the right dose and allowed time for it to take effect, I was pronounced well enough to be discharged. I couldn't do paid work, however, and I didn't work again for the next three years. Instead, I had regular counselling sessions and set myself the goal of getting through just one day at a time.

I was still having flashbacks and nightmares, which meant that my head was filled, waking and sleeping, with horrible images of the child that was me but didn't seem to be me. I felt as though it was my responsibility to watch over that child and my duty to protect her. But I couldn't protect her, because, however hard I tried, I could never reach her. So I was forced to watch the same reel of film playing over and over again, on a continuous loop in my mind, while all the time the hatred I felt for my father continued to grow. He didn't love me and he'd never cared about me, and that knowledge was almost more difficult to try to come to terms with than anything else.

On some days, I couldn't focus on anything for long enough to get a grip on reality at all. Sometimes, I'd sit on the sofa in my flat, holding my hands out in front of me, palms upwards and with their edges touching, and imagine I could see my life slipping away like water between my fingers. I was frightened and tearful, and whenever I tried to visualise my future, all I could see was a dark, empty room.

In time, though, having tumbled, like Alice in Wonderland, to the very bottom of a deep hole into a world of chaos and craziness where nothing made sense, I began to crawl my way up again towards the barely discernible light. I'd often miss my footing and, as I started to slip backwards and was reaching out for something to hold on to, I'd think of Sam and of how, if I killed myself, he might grow up thinking I hadn't loved him. And it was that thought that gave me just enough energy and incentive to keep going.

Gradually – almost imperceptibly at first – I started to feel better. The new dose of medication I was taking helped to suppress the images in my head and, as it did so, it freed up enough space for me to think about other things until, eventually, I was well enough to start doing voluntary work. I became a mentor to young people with learning difficulties – someone they could talk to and go out with – and that's when I realised what I really wanted to do was work with children who'd been abused.

I'd always hated the fact that when I was ill I couldn't think about anything or anyone except myself: the vivid, powerful images in my head simply blotted out everything else. But, as soon as I was well again and could think sensible thoughts, it suddenly seemed really important to me to be able to make a difference.

I became convinced that if I could come to terms with all the terrible things that had happened to me, I could use my own experiences to help children who were suffering in the way I had. Then, one day, I had a sudden flash of understanding and I realised there was no point wishing my childhood had been different and that my father had loved me in the way a father ought to love his daughter. My childhood was over and, however much I might want to do so, I couldn't go back and try to put things right for myself. What I *could* do, though, was help children who were currently going through the sort of things I'd gone through, because I could recognise the pain of abuse when I saw it in their eyes, and I could understand how they felt.

The other blinding, simple truth that came to me at that time was that to be able to help those children, I had to stay well myself. I would never be any use to anyone if I remained a periodically gibbering wreck who had to be carted off from time to time to a psychiatric hospital. The children I wanted to work with needed someone they could trust enough to talk to, someone who could give them hope that they could recover from what had been done to them and lead normal lives.

When I was a teenager, some people – including my mother – used to tell me I was mad, a lunatic, and that only a crazy person would behave in the way I was behaving. And I used to think they were right. It felt as though my actions and reactions were being guided by something that was beyond my control. When I was in

my teens and was drinking and partying every weekend, it must have looked to other people as though I
was thoroughly enjoying myself. Whereas, in fact, I felt
as though I was in a runaway train, which was gather-
ing speed at an alarming rate while I desperately
searched for the brake.

I hadn't known what was wrong with me – although
I knew without any doubt that *something* was – and
I'd longed to have someone I could talk to. But once I
understood why I'd been so unhappy and why I'd
pretended I didn't care about anyone or anything, I
was certain that I could use my own experiences to do
some good. Although it was a daunting prospect, I felt
that if I could help just one young person not to have
to go through what I'd gone through – and what I was
still struggling to come to terms with every day as an
adult in my thirties – everything would have been
worthwhile.

It was the first positive thing that had ever seemed
possible amidst all the many negatives associated with
my father's abuse of me, and as soon as I was well
enough, I signed up to do a college course in social
care.

As a little girl, I'd assumed that all fathers treated
their daughters the same way my father treated me.
You don't even think about your life when you're a
child; it just *is*. So it had been a terrible shock when I

was 12 years old and had finally realised that he – and his friends – had been sexually abusing me. I think that's when doors had started slamming shut in my mind, sealing off the worst of my childhood memories because they were too awful for me to try to make any sense of them. Then, more than ten years later, the birth of my son had triggered the gradual opening of those doors – a process that had proved too much for my mind to cope with.

Over the years, I'd told a few people who were close to me just a little of what my father had done to me, and they all said, 'That's appalling. I simply can't imagine how that must have felt.' So I'd always felt very alone and had often wondered 'Why me?' And then, while I was doing the course at college, I read a book that had an incredible effect on me. It was about a woman who'd been abused as a child, and who felt exactly as I had done. It was a shocking, miserable story, but it struck a chord that was so exciting for me that I wrote to the book's author. I didn't expect a reply, so I was amazed when I received a letter from her almost by return post. And what she wrote changed the way I felt for ever.

It sounds strange to say that discovering there were lots of women – and men – who'd had childhood experiences similar to my own made me feel part of something; but it did. My psychiatrist had been the only person who'd ever seemed able to empathise with the way I felt – and that was only because he'd learned about child abuse by reading about it in textbooks and by hearing stories like my own. And then, through the author of the book I'd just read, I met other women who knew exactly how degraded, damaged and unloved I'd always felt, because they felt the same way too.

Over the next few months, I set up a small local support group for survivors of child abuse and several of us met every week to provide each other with emotional and often practical support. Although the struggle was far from over – and perhaps it never really does end for people who've been abused as children – that was an important turning point for me, and I'll always be grateful to those women for talking to me about their fears and their feelings and for listening when I told them about mine.

They were all really nice people – damaged, as I was, but, without exception, decent human beings. Not one of them was 'bad' or 'worthless', and although they were all still affected – to varying but significant degrees – by what had happened to them, none of them was defined by it. Gradually, the thought began to take root in my mind that perhaps I was just like them – not bad, not useless; just a young woman who'd had a terrible childhood through no fault of her own and who was trying, desperately, to do her best, against all the odds.

Talking to people whose own pain was so great that they were able to cope with hearing about mine was an extraordinary experience. And it was my elation at feeling that they *really* understood what I was saying, as well as a growing sense that a widespread injustice of enormous proportions was being virtually ignored, that prompted me to decide to take my father to court.

People kept telling me how brave I was and how they were behind me 100 per cent; they meant it, of course, and I was buoyed up by their praise and encouragement and by the righteousness of my cause. What I didn't realise, though, was that I wasn't ready to take such a momentous step.

I went to the police – which was something I never thought I'd have the courage to do – and told them my story. I was expecting them to have one of two possible reactions: total disbelief, particularly when I told them who my father was and gave them the names of some of the men who'd abused me; or disgust that I'd allowed something so repellent to be done to me, even though I was just a child at the time. I knew that it would be an ordeal, whatever the outcome, and I had to keep reminding myself that I *had* to speak out, because telling my story might encourage other people to tell theirs, and only when enough victims of abuse were shouting loudly enough would we stand any chance of being heard.

When I arrived at the police station, my heart was thumping erratically, my hands were soaked in sweat and my legs were trembling so violently I could barely walk up the steps to the door. And although I continued to feel as though I was going to be swamped by panic every time I talked about my father's abuse, I was amazed by how sympathetic and supportive the police officers were. I'm sure they'd have been equally compassionate whatever the situation, but what probably helped my credibility was the fact that they'd already started to investigate the activities of my father and several of his friends, and I think they viewed the information I was giving them as an unexpected and very welcome gift.

I had just one condition before I agreed to talk to the policewoman: that no one must know I was giving evidence against my father until the police had put together a case against him and were ready to prosecute him. I knew that if he got wind of what I was doing, he'd bully, browbeat and threaten me until I dropped my accusations against him. He'd boasted to me once of having put some poor man 'six feet under' and although I didn't know if it was true, or just a baseless, veiled threat to make me toe the line at the time, it was certainly something I thought he'd have been capable of – by proxy, at least. True or not, however, it was enough to make me afraid and to wonder if I'd made a terrible, potentially fatal, error by setting out on the path I'd taken. But I was reassured when the policewoman told me that they, too, had every reason to keep their investigations quiet.

I was interviewed on several occasions by the same high-ranking and empathetic policewoman. It was difficult telling a complete stranger about things I hadn't even been able to admit to myself until very recently, but I knew she was trying to make it as easy for me as possible. My mother was interviewed as well, and between us we were able to provide her with some quite detailed information.

Although my father had always been very careful not to put in writing anything potentially recrimina-tory, I still had the one letter he'd written to me and the telephone conversation I'd taped when he'd demanded that I should tell my mother not to pursue him for maintenance payments. Although the tape wasn't directly linked to the accusations I was making against him, the way he spoke on it did illustrate the fact that he wasn't the nice, good-humoured man many people thought he was.

I had various other bits of documented evidence that I gave to the police, and the policewoman asked if I could get a copy of my medical records. She said they'd be useful because they'd corroborate some of the things I'd told her, for example the fact that I'd developed boils as a very young child, and because they included my psychiatrist's reports. So I went to see my doctor and told him what I wanted, although I didn't tell him why.

'That's no problem,' he said. 'I've just a couple of pages here.' He picked up the brown envelope on his desk. 'The rest must be in the file in reception. I'll be back in a minute.'

He got up and walked out of the room, leaving the door open slightly behind him, but when he returned a few minutes later, he looked puzzled.

'It's very odd,' he said, sitting down behind his desk. 'But that's all there is: just those two pages. In fact, even those aren't actually consecutive. One's the latest one, but the other is from some years ago. I can't think what's happened to the rest. It was a pretty substantial file, as I'm sure you know.'

I felt a knot of anxiety tightening around my stomach and the doctor must have noticed the uneasy expression on my face, because he smiled and said, 'Don't worry. We'll track them down. They'll be here somewhere.' Then he shrugged as he added, 'It's a mystery, though.'

However, despite an exhaustive search my medical records never did turn up.

I was told by the doctor's receptionist that there was some confusion about what had happened to them after I'd asked to see them a few years previously.

'But I've never asked to see them before,' I said. 'This is the first time.'

It wasn't until a few days later that I remembered the blank piece of paper my father had got me to sign on the pretext of helping me to sort out the problems with my house. It had happened shortly after the media had begun to investigate his activities, and those of some of his friends, and although I didn't connect the two things at the time, I'd known as soon as I'd written my name that I'd done something foolish. When my father didn't contact the solicitor who'd dealt with the sale of my house, as he'd promised he'd do, I'd resigned myself to never knowing why he'd really wanted my signature on that piece of paper.

But, suddenly, it all made sense. If he'd been afraid that I might say something to the journalist who'd phoned me – either deliberately or accidentally – about how he and his friends had abused me as a child, he might well have wanted to make sure I couldn't back-up my allegations with evidence from my medical records. And all he'd have needed to get hold of them was a piece of paper signed by me – with all the 'blah blah', as he'd called it, filled in by him.

I Remember, Daddy

It seemed like a ridiculously cloak-and-dagger explanation. But I knew the lengths my father was prepared to go to in order to protect his carefully constructed pack of cards from attack. He had a great deal to hide – and a great deal to lose – and he was ruthlessly determined to keep it hidden. He'd been living two parallel lives: one as a successful businessman and pillar of society, and the other centred on his obsession with sex and on his substantial additional income of dubiously earned money. So he'd needed friends in high places to ensure he remained one step ahead of anyone who might set out to drag him down. Which was why, for years, he'd been building a wide-ranging network of useful people. And I was certain he'd have taken whatever steps seemed necessary to ensure that I could never expose and humiliate him – including something as relatively simple as gaining access to my medical records.

Sixteen

I hadn't seen my father for some time when I bumped into him one day in a bar, shortly after my visit to the doctor. He was in his flamboyant persona, the one he adopted in public when there were people there to admire and be amused by him. I hardly listened to what he was saying, however, because I was trying to pluck up the courage to say something myself.

I hated hearing him showing off, telling stories and jokes and being charming. I didn't want to be there with him for a moment longer than I had to, and the anxiety of waiting began to make me feel panicky. Eventually, though, he turned away from the group of people he'd been entertaining and I took a deep breath and told him, in what I hoped sounded like a casual tone, 'I went to my doctor the other day, and it seems that most of my medical records have disappeared, including all the ones from my time in hospital.'

I'd hoped he'd look guilty, or at least uncomfortable, but I should have known better: there was very little anyone could do or say that would discomfort someone as supremely arrogant as my father. He just looked at me with an expression I couldn't read, took a mouthful of his whisky and asked, 'What did you want them for?'

'Oh, I just needed them for something to do with college,' I told him, letting my own eyes slide away from his face and feeling my fingers curl into tight fists.

'Don't worry,' my father said, bending one arm in front of him to look at his watch. 'I'm on the board of directors. I'll be able to get them for you.'

'You're a director of the hospital?' I asked him. 'I didn't know that.'

'Well, there are lots of things you don't know about me.' He laughed and turned away from me, towards his friends.

Nothing happened, of course, and after a few days I phoned him and confronted him about what he'd told me. 'You lied to me,' I said. 'You're not on the board of directors at the hospital.'

'Oh, did you think I said *I* was on the board?' I could hear the sneer in his voice. 'No, I meant that I *know* someone who's on the board. Knowing people in high places can be very useful – for all sorts of reasons. Not least because it often enables me to hear about some things before they even get a chance to happen.'

It sounded as though he was warning me – or perhaps it was a full-blown threat – and I felt my stomach contract with fear.

A few days later, I was contacted by the police and a date was set for me to make my final, official, statement. The interviews had been harrowing. Despite everyone's best efforts, the whole process of telling my story to the police had proved to be as traumatic as I'd thought it would be, and I'd begun to wish I'd never embarked upon it at all. But it did make me feel better knowing that the police believed what I'd told them, and also because it appeared that, at last, my father was going to have to answer for all the terrible things he'd done.

I'd admired the courage of other people I'd heard of who'd spoken out about their experiences of abuse and I was proud to feel that I could now count myself amongst them. Telling my story to the police had taken its toll on my mental well-being and had left me feeling more battered and vulnerable than I'd anticipated.

I Remember, Daddy

But I comforted myself with the thought that perhaps it might help someone else to realise they weren't all alone in the world and that they didn't have to be ashamed because of what someone else had done to them.

And then, one morning, I had a phone call from a journalist.

It was a Saturday and I was at home, washing dishes in the kitchen of my flat, when the phone rang. I reached for the little towel that was looped through the handle on the oven door and carried it with me into the living room as I wiped my hands.

I didn't recognise the voice of the person who spoke to me when I picked up the receiver, but he seemed to know me.

'Hi Katie,' he said. 'Have you got a moment to chat?'

'I'm sorry, I ...' Some sixth sense made me hesitate and I could feel the goose bumps pushing through the skin on my arms.

The man had started to say something, but I interrupted, trying to keep my own voice steady as I asked, 'Who is this?'

'It's Joe,' he answered. 'Joe Kennedy. I work for the local paper.'

I sank into the chair beside the phone, closing my eyes for a moment as I concentrated on fighting my rising sense of nausea. My heart was racing and for a moment all I could hear was the hollow echoing sound of blood pumping in my ears. I struggled to concentrate and to try to think why a journalist might be phoning me at home on a Saturday morning. But all I could come up with were a couple of ridiculously implausible explanations that made no real sense at all.

'Are you still there, Katie?' The man sounded friendly, but I imagined I could hear in his voice the hiss of a snake when he said the letter 's'.

'I don't …' I stopped and inhaled slowly to try to regulate my breathing. 'What do you want? I'm busy at the moment. I can't really talk.'

'Oh, this won't take a minute,' the man assured me cheerfully. 'I just wanted to ask for your confirmation of a few points in relation to what you've been discussing with the police.' He paused for a moment before adding, 'About your father.'

'I can't speak to you,' I almost shouted at him, and then I pressed the disconnect button on the telephone and threw down the receiver as though it had burned my hand.

I walked slowly back into the kitchen, sat at the little breakfast bar looking out over the familiar houses and streets below me, and tried to concentrate on what the journalist had just said to me. My whole body was shaking and my mind was so full of a chaotic jumble of irrational half-thoughts that nothing seemed to make sense.

He couldn't have got hold of any of the information I'd been giving to the police, I told myself. His phone call and questions had just been a lucky shot in the dark. It wasn't possible that he actually *knew* anything, because I'd only spoken to two very senior police officers and they'd promised me that everything I told them would remain strictly confidential until all the statements and documentation had been sent as evidence to the Crown Prosecution Service.

But, however much I tried to convince myself otherwise, I knew that Joe Kennedy was following a story, and that, worst of all, if it was ever splashed across the newspapers, my father would know where the information had come from.

Throughout the morning, my phone rang repeatedly, but I didn't answer it. Instead, I sat in a chair and tried to think. Apart from my mother, almost no one knew that I'd been talking to the police – and the few people who did know were all people I trusted completely. So how had a journalist found out?

During the next few days, I expected to be contacted by the policewoman I'd spoken to. But, when no call came, I phoned the police station and asked to speak to her.

'I had a phone call from a journalist,' I said, as soon as she answered the phone. 'You promised me it would be all right. You promised that no one would know about it until later.'

'I'm so sorry, Katie.' She sounded distracted and wary. 'We had a call from him too. But I just don't know how he found out. I really am sorry.'

'I can't go on with it,' I told her. 'I can't give evidence now. I thought I was strong enough to face it, but I'm not. I don't want to talk to you again, not for a while anyway. Just keep all the stuff I gave you and maybe I'll change my mind in time.'

'Okay. I'm sorry,' she said again, and this time I thought I could hear a note of impatience in her voice.

'I just can't believe how this could have happened,' I said. 'I told you that my father wouldn't hesitate to do something to shut me up, even have me killed if he thought I was going to ruin him, and you promised me that no one would know.'

Even in the state I was in, the claim sounded crazy and melodramatic. But I really didn't know how far my father would be prepared to go to preserve his reputation, or what he was capable of doing. On many occasions when I was a little girl, he'd beaten me with a belt until the skin on my bottom was raw and bleeding and I was sobbing and begging him to stop. And on many occasions I'd seen him punch and kick my mother until she was almost unconscious on the floor. Each time it had been a punishment for having irritated or displeased him. So it didn't take a huge leap of the imagination to believe he might kill someone who threatened to expose him and whose evidence might send him to prison.

'I do understand how you feel,' the policewoman said, although I doubted whether she really did. 'We'll keep everything locked up here until the dust has settled and you let us know what you want to do.'

It was just another empty promise, as it turned out, because when I did ask for the documents, photographs and letters to be returned to me a couple of years later, everything had apparently 'gone missing'.

Not long after I'd been contacted by the journalist, I was visited by a friend of my father.

'He isn't well,' he told me. 'He's in hospital. He's got cancer. He has to have an operation, although I'm afraid the best we can hope for is that it will prolong his life a bit. It doesn't look as though he's likely to survive more than a few months at most. I'm sorry Katie, but your father's dying.'

I wanted to shout in his face, 'Hurray! I'm glad. I'm glad he's finally come up against something he can't control. I'm glad he's going to die. He deserves to suffer for what he's done.' But, for some reason I couldn't understand, I didn't feel glad. What I actually felt like doing was bursting into tears and bawling like a child, because I knew that when my father died, any chance that he might one day love and care about me would die with him.

As well as feeling sad, though, I had a sense of relief knowing that his death would bring to an end a chapter in my life that I might not have to think about any more. And then I felt guilty, partly because I was used to feeling guilty about everything and partly because relief seemed a horrible emotion to have when someone tells you your father is going to die.

Later, however, it became clear that a more appropriate reaction to the news might have been sceptical disbelief, because it turned out that although my father did have an operation, he didn't have cancer at all, and he'd never been in any danger of dying. He'd just seen his pending surgery as an ideal opportunity to try to make me feel sorry for him. Perhaps, like the journalist, he'd somehow got wind of the fact that I'd been talking to the police about him and he thought I'd be so upset that he was going to die that I'd withdraw my accusations against him.

Coincidentally, perhaps, a few days later I was contacted by the wife of a friend of my father. Her husband was a man in a high-profile, influential job, and she wrote in her letter to me, 'I know that you were abused by your father when you were a child, because I heard my husband discussing with him on the phone the other day what they could do to stop you talking to the police. I'd be happy to tell the police about that conversation if you want me to.'

I was grateful to the woman for having written that letter and for her offer of support, but I'd realised by that time that I wasn't strong enough to do battle with my father. I was still reeling from the ordeal of telling my story to the police and then discovering that a journalist had found out what I was doing, and I knew that trying to expose my father and make him accountable for what he'd done was going to take more emotional and mental strength than I'd ever be able to muster.

The woman who wrote to me divorced her husband not long afterwards, and her children publicly corroborated the allegations she made about how he used to beat her up and was violent towards all of them. At the time, though – and despite his children's statements – the man claimed that his wife was crazy, and it wasn't until quite recently that she was finally believed, after he was sacked for 'compromising his professional position'.

Some of my father's friends and people close to him for various reasons *were* exposed from time to time. But, even when he had known links with them, he somehow managed to maintain just a peripheral role in their stories, so that the finger of blame was never pointed squarely in his direction. For years, he'd been systematically building up contacts with people who were, or might prove to be, useful to him. More importantly perhaps, he'd gathered incriminating information about powerful men who were lynchpins in the systems that control all our lives.

The media and the police had already got close to him once before and he'd outsmarted them. So what chance did I have of doing what they had been unable to do? Whatever I wanted to believe about how right ultimately triumphs over wrong, I knew that, in the real world, the Davids rarely overcome the Goliaths and that those who try to do so are often destroyed in the process.

So, instead of doing battle with my father, I concentrated on my college course and the work I was doing with young people who'd been abused. When I was working, I could separate my adult self from myself as a child, forget about my own experiences and focus on the young people whose problems were more current and more urgent than my own. And, gradually, the good days began to outnumber the bad.

There *were* still bad days, though, when I'd think about how much my son had had to put up with in his young life – not least having to witness my sometimes erratic, frightening behaviour when I was ill – and I'd feel guilty. Sam was a wonderful child, and he's grown up to be an amazing young man. But, although he was protected from my illness as much as possible by his father and grandparents, I knew that it must have had an effect on him – which is something I regret deeply to this day. And, on some days when I was feeling low, I'd think that he'd be better off if I were dead.

One day, Sam was staying with me and we were being driven somewhere by my friend Jenny. Sam was sitting at the back of the car and I was in the passenger seat at the front. I'd been feeling anxious and depressed for several days, and I'd started to become obsessed by the thought that I was an obstacle to Sam's chances of being happy. I'd said almost nothing since we'd got into the car, and Jenny had been chatting to Sam over her shoulder, trying to mask my gloomy presence and reassure him that everything was normal and okay.

Suddenly, without any warning, I grabbed the handle of the car door and pushed it open. We were travelling at almost 40 mph at the time and as I tried to twist my legs sideways so that I could throw myself out of my seat on to the road, I heard Sam scream.

Cursing, Jenny swung the car towards the pavement and slammed her foot down hard on the brake.

'What the bloody hell are you trying to do?' she shouted at me, banging the steering wheel with the heels of her hands. 'You could have got us all killed. Is that what you want? Is that what you were trying to do – kill your son and your best friend?'

She turned to reach behind her and touched Sam's knee.

'It's all right, Sam,' she told him. 'Everything's all right now. Your mum was just having one of those moments when she wasn't thinking straight.' She glared at me and then her expression softened and there were tears in her eyes as she said again, to all of us, 'It's all right now.'

But it wasn't really all right at all. I'd started drinking again, and again I was struggling to get through each day. Every morning when I woke up, I just wanted to stay in bed and cry with the disappointment of not having died in my sleep.

I was in a relationship at the time, with Jack, who was the love of my life. But when I was ill, it was too much for anyone to deal with, although I know Jack tried, and I know that he loved me too. I'd told him what my father had done to me when I was a child and he began to hate him with an almost obsessive passion.

Jack knew me better than anyone had ever done and I sometimes thought he understood me more than I understood myself. During the time we were together, he saw all my different personalities – including the aggressive side of me and the little girl I sometimes became when I'd sit in a corner and cry. I'm good at hiding how I really feel and at presenting a calm, confident exterior while inside I'm a quivering wreck of insecurities. But Jack saw the demons beneath the mask and – amazingly – still loved me.

My psychiatrist says I had to learn to hide behind a mask when I was a child, because I had to put on the happy, smiling face of daddy's little girl in public, and conceal the deep distress and misery I really felt. It took me years – in fact, until just a couple of years ago – to come to terms with the realisation that I don't have to be like that: I don't have to hide how I feel all the time, because it doesn't matter if people know that I'm upset.

Jack was a really lovely guy, who was as good to Sam as he was to me. But it seemed almost as though he absorbed some of my distress until, ultimately, the strain of my illness and of not being able to do anything to help me proved too much for him to bear. He became so obsessed with the idea of finding some way to pay my father back for what he'd done that he ended up having a nervous breakdown himself and losing everything he had.

Just before we finally split up, Jack went to stay with his family for Christmas. We'd had a really good relationship for five years and he was the first person I'd been able to talk to openly and honestly. I knew, though, that I was pushing him away – as I always did eventually with people I became close to – and, after he left, I sank into depression and self-hatred. It seemed as though there was a pattern to my life, which was destined always to repeat itself; and I'd reached the point when I knew I couldn't cope any more.

My father was abroad with Gillian, but my brother and his wife had invited the rest of the family to spend Christmas Day with them. Although I'd been invited too, I just dropped in to see Sam and my mother and brother for one last time. I particularly wanted to say goodbye to Sam, although when I got to my brother's house I almost couldn't bear the thought that I'd never see him again. I knew I was doing the right thing, though: Tom's family would look after Sam, and I didn't have anything to offer him, other than the constant worry of knowing that his mother was often ill and deeply unhappy.

Jenny had asked me to have Christmas dinner with her and her family, but I'd said I wasn't feeling great and just wanted to go home.

'I'll be fine,' I told her. 'I just feel a bit low and I don't want to drag anyone else down with me. I need to be alone for a while and then I'll be okay.'

I'd been stockpiling tablets for weeks – the Prozac I took for depression; the temazepam that helped me sleep; the chlorpromazine that stopped me being psychotic; and paracetamol, which never seemed to do very much at all. As soon as I got home, I opened a bottle of wine and I was in the process of drinking it to wash down the large handful of pills I was trying to swallow when the phone rang.

I reached out my hand to lift the receiver, shaking my head and blinking a couple of times as I tried to bring the blurred outline of the telephone into focus.

'Katie?' It was Jenny.

'Yes,' I said, taking a deep breath and trying to sound normal.

'Are you okay, Katie? You sound odd.' Jenny's tone was sharp.

In fact, I felt as though I was fading away, as though my body was disappearing as it grew weaker, and I closed my eyes for a moment and tried to concentrate.

'I'm fine,' I told her. 'Just … I'm just going to have a bath. I'll talk to you later.' Then I put down the telephone and walked slowly and unsteadily up the stairs to the bathroom.

I remember turning on the bath taps and taking off my clothes, but the next thing I was aware of was opening my eyes and finding myself lying in a bed. My heart began to race, and as I moved my arm to touch the throbbing pain in my head, I felt a sharp tug in the skin on the back of my hand. Looking down at it, I realised that I was attached to a drip, and I cried out.

Immediately, a nurse appeared beside me.

'You came very close to succeeding this time,' she said, holding my hand so that she could adjust the needle that was inserted into it and then looking at me with narrowed, appraising eyes.

It turned out that I'd been unconscious and in hospital for two days. Jenny had known what I'd done as soon as she'd heard my voice on the telephone and she'd called an ambulance. When they arrived, the ambulance men had had to break down my front door to get in, and they'd found me, naked and unconscious, on the floor of the bathroom.

As the nurse had said, I'd come very close to killing myself, and I felt weaker and more ill than I'd ever done in my life. I was in hospital for a few days and then in bed at home for a few more, and Jenny refused to speak to me.

When she did finally phone me, she was angry.

'What in God's name were you thinking of?' she almost shouted at me. 'You can't keep doing this, Katie. What about Sam? Don't you ever think of how it affects him? I love you to bits, but I can't do this anymore. I can't just sit here and wait until one day I get the call that tells me you've killed yourself. I know what your father did to you and I know that I can't even begin to imagine how awful it was or how difficult it's made everything for you. But you've *got* to stop this. You've got to stop being so selfish and start thinking about all the people who love you.'

For a moment, it felt as though she'd slapped me across the face; and then I realised she was right. Each time I didn't answer my phone and they wondered if I was just out or was lying unconscious – or already dead – on the floor of my home must have been almost worse for my friends and family than if I'd just gone ahead and killed myself. I knew that I had to make a decision and stick to it: life or death? It was tempting to think of closing my eyes and not having to fight to survive any more. But then I thought of Sam and of Jenny and I knew that, although making the decision to live come what may was the more difficult of the two, it was the one I had to make. And never again did I attempt to take my own life.

Perhaps the very act of deciding made me try harder to put the past behind me – as much as I was able to do so – and to concentrate on having a future. Because, without the safety net of that ultimate means of escape, I *had* to make things work.

Not long after Jack left for good, I met Kevin. I still felt as though I needed a man in my life, and Kevin seemed to be perfect, not least because he was all the things my father wasn't: he didn't drink heavily, he didn't take drugs, he worked hard, had a nice car and his own house but with no debts, and he seemed to have values and a strong moral code that he lived by. In fact, I couldn't really believe that he'd be interested in me at all. But he was, and I thought I'd found the knight in shining armour I'd been waiting for ever since I was a little girl and had first escaped from the miseries of my reality into the fantasy world of books.

Seventeen

I was completely devastated by the break-up with Jack. Because I was so ill again, I'd had to stop working, and it felt as though Kevin had thrown me a lifeline when I thought I was going to drown. He'd just come out of a long-term relationship too, and he was looking for someone to fill the gap in his life. So, really, neither of us should have got involved with anyone on a serious level. Nonetheless, we were married just six months after we met.

I knew immediately that I'd made a huge mistake. Even as I was walking down the aisle at our wedding, I was thinking about Jack and wondering what on earth I was doing marrying Kevin. I went through all the motions and tried to pretend I was happy, but inside I was panicking at the thought of what I'd done and because I knew I was facing the prospect of having to spend the rest of my life with the wrong person. I did think I loved Kevin, though, although I realised later that I was probably just grateful to him for being there when I needed someone, and for having tried to create a protective bubble around me.

After we were married, I still wasn't well enough to work and I'd often sit at home during the day and drink. It was a terrible strain on Kevin, because he never knew what sort of state I'd be in when he got home – drunk or sober, deeply distressed or unreasonably elated. When I was well, I could block out most of the memories of my father for most of the time. But whenever I was ill, they'd all came flooding back and it was as though I really was a child again. Sometimes when that happened, alcohol would prevent the memories tumbling round and round in my head, and sometimes it would just make things worse.

Kevin wanted me to go to Alcoholics Anonymous, but I refused because, despite the fact that I was drinking heavily – sometimes as much as two bottles of wine in a day – I knew I wasn't an alcoholic. Eventually, though, he almost convinced me that I was, and I went along to an AA meeting. When I got there, I felt like an imposter. But that was the way I always felt, except this time it soon became clear to everyone that

I was looking in the wrong place for a solution to my particular problems.

What was really making me so unhappy was that when I was with Jack, I'd thought I was reconstructing a life for myself and doing well. Then he'd become ill and left me and, as well as being devastated because I'd lost him, I'd felt guilty, because I thought that I was responsible for his illness. So I'd tried to commit suicide, but failed; and then Jenny had made me realise how much hurt I was causing to the people who loved me, and it seemed as though I'd been given another chance. I'd been determined not to give up again, but not giving up was proving to be even harder than I'd anticipated. I'd lost Jack; I'd married Kevin when I shouldn't have done so; I hadn't slept for days; I wasn't eating; and I was drinking heavily. Fortunately, though, I still had just enough capacity for rational thought to decide to go to see my doctor.

'I'm going to do something to myself,' I told him. 'I can't go on like this. Every time I think things are getting better, it all goes wrong. There are just so many times I can pick myself up and try again, and I've reached the end now.'

'I think you need to go into hospital,' the doctor said. 'You're obviously exhausted, both mentally and physically, and that always affects you badly. Go in for a few days and have a rest, and then we can think again.'

He leaned forward, placing his elbows on his desk and pressing his fingertips together, and I could see from the look of resignation on his face that he was preparing himself for the verbal battle ahead as he tried to persuade me. So he was surprised when I wiped away the tears from my cheeks with the back of my hand and nodded.

I was in the hospital for a couple of weeks, and this time, because I was so thankful not to have to think for myself for a while and so tired that I could hardly walk from one end of a room to the other, I didn't even think about trying to escape.

Kevin came to see me just once, and by the time I left the hospital, our three-month marriage was over. I'd told him at the start of our relationship about my illness and what had caused it, and he'd insisted that he wanted to take care of me. So I was hurt and upset that he seemed ready to give up so easily, and disappointed that he hadn't been the answer to all my problems, as I'd hoped he'd be. But I did understand how difficult it must have been for him when he began to realise the true extent of what he'd taken on, and I knew that I couldn't really blame him for not comprehending exactly how much effort it was going to involve.

What really hurt more than anything, though, was that I'd always been truthful with Kevin, whereas it turned out that he'd been lying to me.

I Remember, Daddy

I'm sure my drinking and erratic behaviour had been really difficult for him to deal with, but he claimed to my friends and family that I *was* an alcoholic and that that was the sole reason for the breakdown of our marriage. Everyone felt sorry for him, particularly when he said that I'd broken his heart, when in fact the truth was that he'd met someone else shortly after our wedding and they'd discovered while I was in hospital that she was pregnant with his child.

I was devastated when I found out that Kevin had been cheating on me; I felt stupid and duped and I became paranoid at the thought that they'd both been laughing at me behind my back. In reality, though, I think our marriage had been doomed from the outset.

I've always been repulsed by sex and I find even the closeness it involves very difficult to cope with. However, until a couple of years ago, I'd been afraid to be on my own, despite being perfectly content with my own company. I think it was because I felt that I needed to have a partner as affirmation of the fact that I'm lovable – although I never actually believed that I was. So I've always gone straight from one relationship into another, without allowing myself time to take stock and reassess who I am and what I want, which – again, until recently – was something I didn't want to look at too closely, because I was afraid of what I might discover. I was always searching for love, without having any real idea what love is.

After I came out of hospital, I stayed with Jenny for four months. She had her own family to look after, but she took care of me too. And it was because of the promise I'd made to her – that I'd never again try to take my own life – that things began to change in a way I didn't at first understand. Making that promise to Jenny had been like deleting my 'opt-out' clause: without the option of killing myself, I had to make things work and get on with living my life; and if they weren't working and I was becoming ill and unhappy, I had to get help. Somehow, that seemed to simplify things in a way that enabled me to keep looking forward all the time.

I'd been seeing a psychiatrist regularly, and we'd begun to talk about all the things I believed and to revisit the reasons why I believed them. Gradually, I was learning to accept that the wires in my brain were crossed and that they needed to be untangled and reconnected properly. The false connections had occurred as a result of the way my father had treated me and because of what he'd told me repeatedly about myself since I was a very young child: that I was a useless, worthless slut and that the sole purpose in life for women – and for little girls – was to serve the sexual needs of men, whatever those might be. The rational, logical side of my brain knew that the things my father had told me weren't true, and as the emotional side learned to accept that too, I seemed to turn a corner.

Six months after I'd had to stop working, I rented a place of my own, went back to work and started doing really well – well enough, eventually, not to have to take the medication I'd been reliant on for almost 18 years. Perhaps most importantly of all, though, I stopped thinking about my father and I stopped having flashbacks and seeing images of the past.

When I was a child, I was pushed from pillar to post, and as a teenager I did all the wrong things – drinking and smoking and even, for a while, stealing – so that I could easily have gone too far down the wrong road to have been able to turn back. I think it was fortunate that the drugs that are so freely available now weren't around when I was young. If they had been, I might well have chosen that path to self-destruction, because I hated my life as a teenager and I didn't know why.

It's almost as though I've been trying for years to revisit my childhood and find out what I did to deserve all the terrible things that happened to me. Finally, though, I've accepted that I *didn't* deserve them, and that my childhood can't be changed. There's no point going over and over it endlessly in my mind, trying to make sense of it, because it doesn't make sense. What happened to me was actually the result of my father's problems – whatever they were. I was, purely and simply, a completely innocent bystander, a film extra, in the life of someone who is sick, perverted and infinitely self-indulgent.

Just over a year ago, I was offered a really good job working with teenagers with behavioural problems, many of whom have been abused. It would mean leaving my home town, moving three hours' drive away from Sam and Jenny and from my safety net of friends whose support I've always relied on. I was scared by the prospect, but I accepted the job, and I'm really glad I did. I'm proud of myself for taking that final step into my future.

From the time when I first started remembering, I could see in my mind the child I used to be and it was as though the child I was seeing was someone else, someone who needed my help, but I couldn't help her. Now, though, I know that I *can* help other children who have suffered abuse and who are angry and confused and just want to lash out and make people feel the same pain that they're trying to bury deep inside themselves.

When I was a teenager, I'd already suppressed the memories of the abuse I'd suffered as a child, so I didn't know what was wrong with me. I often wished

I had someone I could talk to who might help me to create some sort of order in my mind and reassure me that I wasn't mad or bad. Unfortunately, there wasn't anyone for me to confide in, but if I can be that someone for the young people I work with, I'll feel that some good has come out of all the evil that was created by my father.

It took me 40 years to break the chains my father had bound around me so tightly. But I've done it at last, and I know that, in doing it, I've also broken the control he'd exerted over me since I was two years old.

I know that 'the past is always with us'; but that doesn't mean it has to haunt us or that we have to remain under its shadow. We can choose to move forward and *use* our past experiences rather than allowing them to have power over us. Even so, I used to worry about how I might react if I was ever faced with some unexpected reminder of my childhood, which was a question that was answered recently when I had an experience that, not very long ago, would have sent me into a rapid, irreversible nosedive towards regression.

I'd gone to court to support a young person who was giving evidence against a man who'd sexually abused her and two other girls. As I sat beside her, she constantly clasped and unclasped her hands, and her misery and distress seemed almost like something solid that I could have reached out and touched. She was white-faced and shaking, a slight girl who, although in her early teens, still seemed to have the thin, fragile body of a child. I could imagine how terrified she was, and I admired her enormously for having had the courage to agree to give evidence against her abuser.

Suddenly, there was a flurry as everyone got to their feet, and I looked up to see the judge, archaically resplendent in his wig and robe, walk in through a door at the side of the courtroom. I gasped and could immediately sense the tremor of anxiety that ran through the body of the girl beside me. She glanced quickly towards me and I nodded and smiled without turning my head, hoping she would take it to mean that everything was okay. Then I reached out to grasp the back of the wooden pew in front of me as I was engulfed by a wave of nausea. Because the judge who'd entered the courtroom with such self-assured solemnity was a friend of my father and a man who'd abused me in my home when I was a little girl.

The judge sat down on the high-backed chair in the centre of the raised dais that faced into the courtroom, and we all sat down too. He scanned the room for a moment, then picked up a piece of paper from the long wooden desk in front of him, examined it and looked up again. And in the split-second while he held my gaze, I knew he'd recognised my name and realised who I was.

My heart was racing and the palms of my hands were sticky with sweat, but I forced myself to concentrate my attention on the girl sitting beside me. *She* was what mattered now; not me, or the child I used to be, or something that had happened years ago.

The judge never looked in my direction again. His expression was appropriately stern as he listened while the case unravelled, and suitably sympathetic when the girl whispered her answers to the questions she was asked. Then he sentenced the paedophile abuser to five years in prison – which, everyone later agreed, seemed a relatively lenient sentence for someone who'd sexually abused three little girls.

I felt – not for the first time in my life – like Alice in Wonderland; as though I was in a surreal, dream-like world, sitting in a bizarre courtroom where nothing was what it appeared to be, while the Queen of Hearts dispensed summary injustice. But the important thing was that I'd coped. I'd focused on what mattered and provided the girl with the support she needed, and the tightrope on which I was walking had barely wobbled.

Although I still occasionally have bad days, when just getting out of bed seems to require an enormous amount of effort, they're rare now. And I know I can avoid them occurring at all if I make sure I get enough sleep and don't get overtired. I don't self-harm and I'm no longer afraid of my father. I'd been frightened of him my entire life, ever since I was a tiny girl; and then, one day, the fear seemed simply to evaporate – as though I'd snapped my fingers and it had gone.

However, although I'm no longer afraid of him, I'm sure there are many people who are, not least because he has damning evidence that could ruin the careers and reputations of some very influential men in highly respected professions, were it ever to come to light. Mostly, it's evidence related to their sexual activities, and I'm sure that they're all very aware of what my father sometimes told me: 'If I go down, I'll take the whole lot of them with me.'

Nemesis has almost caught up with my father on a couple of occasions. But even fate doesn't seem to be able to break through the protective barrier he's constructed around himself so carefully over the years. Like almost all the men who enjoyed his parties and who had sex with me or with other young people, maintaining the myth of their good reputations is far more important to them than all the lives they've damaged and, in some cases, ruined completely. So my father knows he's safe.

I'd like to think that he sometimes has anxious moments when he wonders whether I'll ever decide to go back to the police and provide them with the evidence they need to take action against him, but I doubt if he loses much sleep over the thought. And he'd be right not to, because although I hate the idea that he'll never have to answer for what he's done, I know that I need to move on with my life, and to do that I have to turn my back on my father in every respect and look forward.

It seemed that the only person my father was ever afraid of was his mother, who, ironically, was also the only person I think he's ever really loved. I asked him once *why* he was the way he was and he told me – in an uncharacteristically unguarded moment – that when he was a little boy, his mother used to make him wear a dress and everyone used to laugh at him. I think that when my father was born, his parents had just lost a little girl, who'd died from some illness, so I assume that had something to do with it. Whatever the reason, he says he swore that, one day when he grew up, he'd make everyone pay for having mocked him and he'd ensure that no one ever laughed at him again. 'I was determined to get the last laugh,' he told me. And I suppose he feels that he has.

If the story he told me is true, the damage his mother's actions caused to his psychological development was inadvertent. Whereas he systematically and deliberately damaged many lives, including my mother's and my own – which seems an unnecessarily vicious way of getting the last laugh.

My grandmother told me once that one summer, when she and my grandfather were staying in the house by the coast, there was a knock at the door in the middle of the night and she opened it to find my father standing there. He was drunk and wearing high-heeled shoes, a feather boa and make-up, and he was with a young woman in a very short skirt. My grandmother was furious with him and said, 'What the hell are you doing? You look bloody ridiculous! Get out of here!' So perhaps it was after that incident that he turned against her, and maybe it was because of her criticism of him that he later refused to help her when she didn't have enough money to heat the miserable, damp flat she was living in all alone.

I know that my father was determined to shake off the memory of the boy from the poor council estate he used to be, and to become a wealthy, successful and respected businessman. It was an ambition in which he succeeded. But, despite outward appearances, it was as though there always remained something rotten inside him, something tainted that he could never quite shake off – although I'm not sure he ever tried. It was something that prevented him ever becoming a decent man and that attracted to him as friends other men who were psychologically unstable, for whatever reason.

I Remember, Daddy

There must be reasons why my father behaved in the way he did, why he despised women and was incapable of loving even the people who loved him. And I've often wondered what they are. But I don't really care any more. He's had his life and he's made his choices; and at last, now that I've stepped out from under the shadow he cast on *my* life, I'm free to make my choices too.

When I was a child, he'd always get up early on weekdays and be dressed and out of the house before I was awake; and he'd often come home after I was in bed. At the weekends, he'd play tennis in the mornings and have lunch in the pub with friends before coming home to have a bath or a nap with me. Then he'd be off out again, often with my mother. So, when he was at home, he was either drunk or in bed; I don't remember him ever being completely sober.

I can remember times when he was funny, though, and sometimes he could even be quite affectionate as he passed through one of the early stages of drunkenness. I have one enduring memory of a party when he danced with me and cuddled me, like a normal dad would do. But then he'd drink some more, and as soon as everyone else had left the house, his good humour would turn to spiteful aggression and he'd be transformed into an unsmiling, violent, frightening bully.

I heard recently that he'd given a talk to help raise money for a charity, and I laughed out loud. Because, as I think I've already mentioned, he *hates* people who need charity – and black people, Arabs (in fact, 'foreigners' of any sort), people who live in council houses, religion, particularly Catholicism …

I know that when he dies there'll be a huge memorial service for him and everyone will say what a wonderful, charismatic, caring man he was. But there'll be dozens – if not hundreds – of people who'll know he wasn't, and many of them will sigh with relief when he's gone.

I don't know how I'll feel when that time comes. Perhaps there's a part of me that will be sad; maybe I'll mourn the loss of my father – although, in reality, I think I did that many years ago. The truth is that what he did to me ruined years of my life. I won't ever forgive him for that, and I certainly won't ever forget about it again. He controlled my past, but I refuse to allow him to control my future.

When the memories started to return, I didn't want to remember. But I know now that if I hadn't, I'd always have felt guilty without ever understanding why. I needed to be able to work through the problems my father created in my life, even though doing so caused me unspeakable anguish and distress and came close to destroying me. The road to recovery was long and I made slow, often painful, progress. There were many occasions when I thought I wasn't going to make it to the end. But I did make it, and at last I can move on and use my experiences to try to help young people whose lives have been similarly damaged.

When I was a little girl, I used to lie in my bed every single night, waiting and wondering. Would my father come into my room and do things to me? Or would he come in and lift me out of my bed and carry me upstairs? And if he did take me upstairs, who would do the things to me then? Occasionally, he didn't come, and I'd fall asleep, still waiting. I spent my childhood waiting, and it sometimes seemed to be the worst thing of all. In some ways, it was almost better to get a beating from my father, because once he was actually beating me, I knew it would soon be over and, for a while at least, I wouldn't have to wait and wonder when it was going to happen.

It was as though there was always someone standing behind me, picking with their fingers at a balloon so that it made a horrible, tight, squeaky noise, while I waited fearfully for it to burst. And now, finally, all these years later, it feels as though I've swung round, snatched the balloon from their hands and burst it myself – and now the waiting is over.

People who know what my father did to me sometimes say, 'Don't worry. He'll get his come-uppance.'

But I think he probably won't. He always wanted to *be* someone – although I'm sure that no one would ever have set out to be the man he became – and now that he *is* someone, maybe he'll get away with it all. I hope, though, that at least his dreams are haunted by the terrible things he's done.

I used to wonder why he'd done those things to me, and for a long time – when I believed that bad things only happen to bad people – I accepted his assertion that they were somehow my fault. I realise now, though, that something very bad must have happened to him to make him the person he became, and part of me would like to be able to say I feel sorry for him. But that wouldn't be true. I don't feel sorry for him because, whatever happened to him, he had a choice, as we all do, and he chose to be a bad person – and that's his fault.

Who knows what my father thinks when he stands alone and looks at his reflection in the mirror – although it doesn't really matter, because this isn't his story; it's mine. The telling of it has sometimes been difficult, but if it gives hope to just one person who was abused as a child or who's struggling to overcome their past for some other reason, then it has all been worthwhile.

Perhaps I had to hit rock bottom before I could really start to get better. I know that I'm lucky, because

I Remember, Daddy

I've got friends I love and who really care about me, and I've got my son. Never a day passes when I don't think about Sam and bless the day he was born. I still feel guilty about what he had to go through because of me. But I think, remarkably, he's always understood that I was ill and that I'd have been there for him all the time if I'd had the choice. He knows my father abused me when I was a child, and he never asks about him or even mentions his name.

Perhaps one of the things I *did* get right, though, was choosing a good father for Sam, because he's been very fortunate to have had Tom and his family to take care of him and to love him the way they've always done. I believe Sam has always known how much I love him too, and that he's the most important thing in my life. He's 20 now; he's a really lovely young man and he has a good job that he enjoys and is making a success of – which, considering the fruitcake his mother has been over the years, is quite an achievement.

As well as Sam, I've got Jenny to thank for the fact that I'm still here. We've known each other since we were 12 years old; she's my rock and my dearest friend, and there have been many times when, quite literally, I couldn't have coped without her. Now that I live so far away from her, I miss her and text her almost every day, and I do wish that she was here with me.

On the other side of the coin, however, is the fact that missing the people I love is a constant reminder to be proud of the way I'm coping and of how far I've come. I'm proud, too, of having achieved my ambition of working in childcare, which, although often distressing, has proved to be as rewarding and satisfying as I'd hoped it would be.

I'm contented now, and I didn't think that was something I was ever going to be able to say. I've learned, at last, to stop looking over my shoulder at the past and instead to look forward to the future I know that I can create for myself. I've discovered that I'm stronger than I ever realised, and I'm determined that who I am and what I do with my life will not be defined in any negative way by what happened to me as a child. I'm immensely fortunate to have people who love me and who I can rely on and, finally, I've learned to accept and be grateful for their love without feeling guilty and undeserving of it.

I love my job, too, and I appreciate the satisfaction it gives me of feeling that I'm making a difference, however small. Most of the young people I work with have suffered abuse – physical, sexual, mental and/or emotional – often at the hands of one or both of their parents or another close family member; and when you understand how bewildered, hurt and angry they are, it's hardly surprising that their behaviour is sometimes challenging. I know they're not bad people, any of them, despite what they may believe about themselves; and they're certainly not worthless or useless. By helping them to see that, and by being there if they need someone to talk to as they struggle to make sense of the chaos of their emotions, I feel as though something positive has evolved from what used to seem so irredeemably hopeless.

I've come a long way, and I'm proud to be moving forward in my life – against all the odds. If things sometimes go wrong for me in the future, I'll know that it isn't because of what happened to me in the past, or because I'm a bad person; it's just that, sometimes, things happen to us all – good and bad. And I can deal with that.

Ultimately, remembering made me stronger and, most importantly of all, it made me realise that I don't have to be afraid anymore.